Peace Corps
The Great Adventure

*The Peace Corps acknowledges the special efforts of
Penny Anderson, Michael Chapman, John Coyne,
Patricia Cunningham, Janet Getchell, Rose Green,
Wendy Henderson, and Nancy Scott
in the selection, editing, design,
and production of this book.*

*The Peace Corps also expresses its appreciation to
the Returned Peace Corps Volunteers of Wisconsin/Madison
and the following photographers for permission
to use the photos that appear on the cover of this book:*

*Front cover
Guatemala photo by Janet Getchell
Ethiopia and Nepal photos by Scott Faiia*

*Back cover
Pakistan photo by Christina G. Boyd*

*For more information about the Peace Corps,
please call 800-424-8580
or
visit our web site at
http://www.peacecorps.gov*

*Library of Congress Catalog
No. 97-68135*

ISBN 0-9644472-2-3

Peace Corps: The Great Adventure

The Peace Corps wishes to express its appreciation to the authors and publishers for permission to reprint the following: "Miss Lillian Sees Leprosy for the First Time" by Jimmy Carter, © 1995 by Jimmy Carter, from *Always a Reckoning*; "Finding My Village" by Charles R. Baquet III, © 1997 by Charles R. Baquet III, from *American Visions*; "'Magic' Pablo" by Mark Brazaitis, © 1997 by Mark Brazaitis, from *RPCV Writers & Readers*; "So This Is Paris" by Kathleen Coskran, © 1994 by Kathleen Coskran, from *RPCV Writers & Readers*; "To Peel Potatoes" by John P. Deever, © 1996 by John P. Deever, from *RPCV Writers & Readers*; "Save Johnny" by Paul Eagle, © 1997 by Paul Eagle, from *RPCV Writers & Readers*; "Development is Down This Road" by Abigail Calkins, © 1992 by Abigail Calkins, from *RPCV Writers & Readers*; "The Joy of Digging" by Mike Tidwell, © 1990 by Mike Tidwell, from *The Ponds of Kalambayi: An African Sojourn*, published by Lyons and Burford; "The Right Way to Grow Tomatoes" by Karen DeWitt, © 1997 by Karen Dewitt, from *RPCV Writers & Readers*; "Rose Garden Redux" by John Coyne, © 1996 by John Coyne, reprinted by permission of the author; "To Be a Volunteer" by Thomas J. Scanlon, © 1997 by Thomas J. Scanlon, from *Waiting For The Snow: The Peace Corps Papers of a Charter Volunteer*, published by Posterity Press.

September 1997

TABLE OF CONTENTS

INTRODUCTION
by Mark D. Gearan

Since 1961, when President John F. Kennedy called upon every American to give something back to our country, nearly 150,000 Americans have responded to his challenge to serve by joining the Peace Corps. Through their spirit of service, their commitment to improve the human condition at the most basic level, and their willingness to share their skills and ideals with the people of developing countries, these men and women have made the Peace Corps one of our country's most successful and enduring experiments in public service. People in more than 130 countries have come to know the Peace Corps as an organization that sends some of America's finest citizens to help the people of the developing world build a better future. At the same time, Peace Corps Volunteers have helped to strengthen the bonds of friendship and understanding between Americans and the people of the countries where they served.

Each year, tens of thousands of Americans contact the Peace Corps seeking information about how to become a Volunteer. They come from every social, political, economic, ethnic, and cultural background, and their reasons for joining the Peace Corps vary just as widely. Many people want to bring their skills in health, education, the environment, economic development, or agriculture to help solve some of the most intransigent problems that confront people and communities in developing countries. Others want to become a Volunteer in order to experience the extraordinary cross-cultural opportunity of living and working at the grass-roots level in another country for two years, learning a new language, and becoming immersed in an entirely different culture.

The essays that appear in this book offer diverse and interesting perspectives on what for many is the "great adventure" of being a Peace Corps Volunteer. As you will read, service in the Peace Corps has had a significant impact on the lives of people who have served as Volunteers in the 1960s, 1970s, 1980s, and 1990s. Moreover, many of the essays in this book offer an answer to the questions most often asked by those who are thinking about joining the Peace Corps: "What is it like to be a Peace Corps Volunteer?" and "What will my job be?"

We are particularly fortunate to include in this collection a poem that President Jimmy Carter wrote about his mother, Miss Lillian Carter, who served as a Peace Corps Volunteer in India in the late 1960s. In addition, Secretary of Health and Human Services Donna Shalala has contributed a moving remembrance of how she learned of President Kennedy's assassination while she was serving as a Volunteer in Iran. Ambassador Charles R. Baquet III, who served as a Volunteer in Somalia and who is the first African American to hold the job of Deputy Director of the Peace Corps, reflects on how the Peace Corps influenced him and his career.

We are also honored to include in this book an inspiring speech by Secretary of State Madeleine Albright about the importance of America's engagement in the world and the role that Peace Corps Volunteers continue to play in building peace, understanding, and friendship. Former Congressman and White House Chief of Staff Leon Panetta has contributed an essay that conveys the pride that he continues to feel about his son's service as a Peace Corps Volunteer in Ecuador.

Finally, we have included excerpts from a speech by former Peace Corps Director Loret Miller Ruppe, who was appointed by President Ronald Reagan to head the Peace Corps in 1981. By the time she left in 1989, she had become (and still remains) the agency's longest-serving Director. Although she passed away in 1996, Director Ruppe left behind an extraordinary legacy of leadership, vision, and accomplishment at the Peace Corps. She touched the lives of many Peace Corps Volunteers, and because she embodied the finest traditions of service, the Peace Corps is proud to have established the Loret Miller Ruppe Lecture Series, which provides a forum for distinguished individuals to contribute to public discussion about issues that bear on the Peace Corps' mission. The Peace Corps has also established the Loret Miller Ruppe Fund for the Advancement of Women. This fund, which was founded with a generous contribution from Director Ruppe's estate, will be devoted to assisting small, community-based projects that are aimed at promoting the role and needs of women in the developing world.

In response to a recent survey of returned Volunteers who have served in the Peace Corps at some point since 1961, ninety-four percent of those surveyed said they would still make the same decision to join the Peace Corps, and ninety-three percent said they would recommend Peace Corps service to others. There are few organizations, public or private, that can claim this level of success. But this is just one measure of the Peace Corps' success. As the stories in this book demonstrate, Peace Corps Volunteers have made a difference in the lives of many people around the world. That is why we say that serving as a Peace Corps Volunteer is "the toughest job you'll ever love." As you'll see from these stories, it's also a "great adventure."

Mark D. Gearan is the Director of the Peace Corps.

Miss Lillian Sees Leprosy for the First Time

When I nursed in a clinic
near Bombay,
a small girl, shielding
all her leprous sores,
crept inside the door.
I moved away,
but then the doctor called,
"You take this case!"
First I found a mask,
and put it on,
quickly gave the child
a shot and then, not well,
I slipped away to be alone
and scrubbed my entire body red and raw.

I faced her treatment every week with dread and loathing
—of the chore, not the child.
As time passed, I was less afraid and managed not to
turn my face away.
Her spirit bloomed as sores began to fade.
She'd raise her anxious,
searching eyes to mine
to show she trusted me.
We'd smile and say
a few Marathi words,
and then reach and
hold each other's hands.
And then love grew between
us, so that, later
when I kissed her lips
I didn't feel unclean.

Jimmy Carter

President Carter's mother, Lillian, served as a Peace Corps Volunteer
in India from 1967-69.

Washington, D.C.

THE LEGACY OF THE NEW FRONTIER
by Madeleine K. Albright

The Peace Corps was based on core convictions: that America's future would be linked to that of developing nations; that progress in those nations could best be achieved not simply through the transfer of money, but through the teaching of skills; and that the role of Americans in the world is not to sit back and put our feet up, but to lead.

In those early days, some of the nation's ablest minds were harnessed to design a Peace Corps that would work. Young people responded eagerly to J.F.K.'s challenge to serve. The first Volunteers were welcomed warmly in developing countries around the world. Soon, even the skeptics were converted by the enthusiasm with which the enterprise was launched. In the words of Senator Barry Goldwater:

"At first, I thought the [Peace Corps] would be advance work for a group of beatniks, but this is not so . . . I have been impressed with the . . . young men and women going into it . . . [and] I know that the . . . overseas experience will be . . . rewarding. I'll back it all the way."

That tradition of broad bipartisan support for the Peace Corps has continued to this day. But the future of this institution and of the principled activism that it represents is not assured.

Today, there are many who suggest that the problems of developing nations and peoples need not concern us now that the Cold War is over; or that the poverty these fragile nations confront is simply not soluble; or that violence is so deeply ingrained in some cultures that social progress is too much to expect.

There are others who despair not of the world around us, but of America itself. They argue that we have turned inward and that the patriotic spirit summoned by President Kennedy has diminished or turned sour. These arguments cannot be lightly dismissed. The trend towards isolation is greater now than it has been in seventy years. If our response is simply to ignore that trend or to patronize the emotions underlying it, we will invite disaster.

To borrow a sound bite from this political season, we

must do to isolationism what some would have us do to the tax code—drive a stake through it, kill it, bury it, and be sure it does not rise again. For if we allow this cancer to spread, we will embolden our enemies, unnerve our friends, weaken ourselves, and betray our children.

Let us begin with this truth: those who insist that Americans should devote primary attention to problems at home are not wrong; they are right. Our position in the world depends on the vigor of our economy, the vitality of our institutions, the unity of our people, and the clarity of our moral vision. But a second truth is that challenges overseas cannot be ignored. Today, our fundamental aims are not opposed by another superpower. Nuclear weapons no longer target our homes. But, although the Cold War is over, a viper's nest of lesser perils remains.

If you doubt that, consider the rise of international criminal cartels, the dispersal of nuclear and other advanced arms, the poisoning of our environment, the mobility of epidemic disease, the persistence of ethnic conflict, and—as we have seen too often in recent days—the deadly and cowardly threat of terror.

It has been true throughout this century. It should be self-evident now. We Americans can never be secure in isolation; the modern world simply does not permit that. It may be reassuring to pull the covers up over our heads and to pretend that what happens far from our shores does not matter. But the truth is that it does matter when America takes the lead in supporting the peacemakers over the bomb-throwers in tinderbox regions such as the Middle East, Northern Ireland, and the Balkans.

It matters when we gain a global consensus, as we did last year, to extend the treaty barring additional nations from developing nuclear weapons. That is a gift to the future.

It matters when President Clinton organizes an international coalition that restores democracy to Haiti, ending the horrible violations of human rights there, enabling the Peace Corps to return, and allowing Haitians to build a decent life at home, rather than risk their lives at sea.

It matters when, through a combination of public and private actions, the rate of infant mortality in the developing world since John Kennedy's time is cut in half, the life expectancy almost doubles, and the rate of child immunization rises to more than eighty percent.

It matters when the Fourth World Conference on Women, heeding the eloquence of America's First Lady, approves a blueprint for action to end discrimination and stop violence against women and girls.

It matters when America takes the initiative at the United Nations and around the world to halt the transfer of anti-personnel land mines, the "Saturday night special" of modern war. You who have been to Angola, Cambodia, Mozambique, or El Salvador know: offer help and the first thing people ask for is prosthetic devices. You who may have siblings or children now on duty in Bosnia understand: for the sake of us all, we must end the scourge of land mines, and we must do it now.

Finally, it matters when we are true to John Kennedy's promise—and the promise of the Peace Corps—to help the deserving help themselves.

The good news, in which the Clinton Administration strongly believes, is that human security, prosperity, and freedom are dynamic, not finite. They are dynamic and alive. If we till the soil and plant the seeds, the seeds will grow and bear rich fruit. That is why an organization like the Peace Corps is absolutely essential. Its very purpose is to cultivate, nourish, and sustain our faith—our faith in each other as human beings and, at the same time, our faith in ourselves.

Madeleine K. Albright is the United States Secretary of State.

Carmel Valley, California

MY GREATEST ACCOMPLISHMENT
by Leon Panetta

I am often asked what I consider to be my greatest accomplishment in life: representing my constituents in California for sixteen years in the U.S. House of Representatives; holding the job of Chairman of the House Budget Committee; or serving as President Clinton's Director of the Office of Management and Budget and as his White House Chief of Staff.

All of these jobs allowed me to be a part of significant debates about important national issues, and to help find solutions to many of the problems that confront our country and our communities. In the process, I hope that I was able to make a positive difference in the lives of Americans.

But while my career in Washington meant a great deal to me, the biggest accomplishment in my life has been to raise three outstanding young men. My wife, Sylvia, and I tried to instill in our sons a set of values that would give them a sense of civic responsibility and commitment to service. One sign that we had some success came when our son, Chris, decided to join the Peace Corps.

When Chris told us of his plans to become a Peace Corps Volunteer, like many parents, we paused to think about what this would mean: our son would be going overseas not for a week-long spring break or even to study for a semester abroad. Chris' decision to join the Peace Corps meant that he would be leaving us for two years to serve in a small community in a distant country we had never seen.

Our initial hesitation, however, was only brief. Sylvia and I had known, of course, about the Peace Corps and the great tradition of service it represents. I can still recall the excitement that was generated across our country when President Kennedy announced its establishment. Over the years, we had read about the extraordinary work that Peace Corps Volunteers had done around the world. We had long admired the spirit of idealism that Volunteers embody and respected their many contributions to the cause of peace and progress. We knew that the Peace Corps was one of our government's most successful programs.

But most of all, we knew that joining the Peace Corps was important to Chris, and we were eager to support him.

Chris' service as a Peace Corps Volunteer in Kenya from 1986 to 1988 was an extraordinary experience for him. His two years in Kenya were filled with both success and frustration. Learning a new language, adjusting to the complexities of an entirely different culture, and leaving behind his family and friends posed new challenges for him. But Chris often reminds me that what he learned from the people in his community, the close friendships that he established, the sense of accomplishment and the adventures that he experienced made all of the challenges seem small in retrospect. Although he's been back home for almost ten years, Chris' time in the Peace Corps is still, and I think always will be, an important part of his life.

Chris came back from Kenya an even stronger person than he was when he left. Sylvia and I marveled at how he had grown, both professionally and personally. And while there were many times during those two years that we missed having him at home, we are grateful that the Peace Corps afforded our son such an opportunity.

There is also something intangible that is part of being the parent of a Peace Corps Volunteer: to see your child assume the responsibility of being a public servant and make a difference in the lives of people is a source of enduring pride. Sylvia and I are fortunate that all of our children carry with them that same spirit of service. And that is my greatest accomplishment.

Leon Panetta was a U.S. Representative from California's 16th (now 17th) congressional district from 1977 until 1993, when he was appointed by President Clinton to be the Director of the Office of Management and Budget. From 1994 to 1997, he served as the White House Chief of Staff. He and his wife live in Carmel Valley, California.

Iran, The Near East

WELCOME TO THE "PACE" CORPS
by Donna E. Shalala

I still think of myself as a Peace Corps Volunteer. The Peace Corps experience began for me in the spring of my senior year of college. I remember walking across the beautiful, small, midwestern campus of Western College for Women to get my mail. The telegram—the first telegram I had ever gotten in my life—came along with one rejection and one acceptance to law school. I remember it had a misspelling, "Welcome to the Pace Corps." The decision about what to do—law school or the Peace Corps—was easy. I was a child of my generation. I was a Kennedy Kid.

My family opposed my going into the Peace Corps. My

dad even offered me a car as a bribe not to join. My Lebanese grandmother, however, finally settled the issue. "Donna," she said, "is going to the Old Country—she'll be fine." As I left for Iran she pressed into my hand a letter written in classical Arabic. "Give this to the head man in the village," she whispered.

When I arrived in Moli Sani, a small Arab village, I gave the letter to the local *mullah*. It turned out that my grandmother had written, "This is to introduce the child of a great sheikh in Cleveland, Ohio. Please put her under your protection." Like my family, the wise *mullah* took my grandmother's order seriously.

I was assigned to teach at the Agricultural College at Ahwaz, and it was a challenge. At our first faculty meeting, the Dean went around the room and called the names of all the men, including the male Peace Corps Volunteers. He skipped me. I went to see him in his office and asked him why he hadn't called my name. He said that he didn't know what to say. He had no experience calling on female teachers.

I took it one day at a time. There were women students who needed my attention, so I became an Instructor of English and Dean of Women.

The women, too, were struggling. Most of the girls their age were already married. Classes were integrated, but the girls and boys sat apart. Gradually we made progress—we created supervised time, including sports, where the students could meet and talk. Two years later there were friendships as well as engagements, not in the traditions of American colleges, but in an Iranian version.

There were other signs of progress. The dean eventually began calling on me at faculty meetings, and the male students, while they still stuck weird things in my teacher's desk, became much more respectful.

My college was located next to a traditional mud village. One day a college guard, who lived in the village, became ill. I asked about him and found out that he had not been to our health clinic because his salary was too low. And he clearly needed to go to a hospital.

I asked our dean to help, and I'll never forget what he said to me: "The problem with you Americans is that you care about individual human life."

That was true, I said. And I persisted and told him that good workers needed good health care. Finally, we got the guard to the hospital.

The day that I remember most vividly in the Peace Corps was the day after President Kennedy was assassinated. Depressed, some friends and I were not in the mood to deal with the local beggar when he approached us. But then with a sad smile, he said, "No money. I want to tell you how sad we all are that your young president was assassinated."

There, in a remote town halfway around the world, a distraught young Peace Corps Volunteer and a beggar embraced and cried together over the death of President Kennedy.

Years later, looking back at my Peace Corps service, I realized that a wise *mullah*, an insensitive Dean, and students struggling to preserve a traditional society in a modern age had changed me forever. I had become a citizen of the world. Because of the Peace Corps, I was sensitive to cultural differences, comfortable sitting on mud floors and talking to tribal leaders, respectful of the role of religion, and in awe of the struggles of desperately poor people who manage to maintain their dignity and care for their children.

For me, it has been quite a journey, one that began thirty-five years ago with a letter welcoming me to the "Pace" Corps. I am proud to say that I still think of myself as a Peace Corps Volunteer.

Donna E. Shalala (Iran 1962-64) was appointed by President Clinton to be the U.S. Secretary of Health and Human Services in 1993. As Chancellor of the University of Wisconsin-Madison from 1988-93, she was the first woman to head a Big Ten University. She also served as President of Hunter College of the City University of New York for eight years, and as Assistant Secretary of Housing and Urban Development during the Carter Administration.

Guatemala,
Central America

"MAGIC" PABLO
by Mark Brazaitis

P ablo and I liked to play "Let's imagine." We'd be
walking down the street, a basketball cradled under
one of our arms. Clouds would be gathering in the
east, as they tended to do in early evening. A light rain—
chipi-chipi is what everyone in town called it—might even
be falling.

"Let's imagine," Pablo would say, "that Michael Jordan
is walking with us."

He would smile. "What would these people say?" he
would ask, pointing to the women in dark blue *cortes* and
white *húipiles,* the native dress in this town in the northern
mountains of Guatemala. "What would they do?"

"They'd be amazed," I'd say. "They wouldn't know what to do."

Pablo would agree. "They'd probably run. But we'd just keep walking down the street, the three of us, to the basketball court."

Then Pablo would ask, "And how would we divide the teams?"

"Michael Jordan versus the two of us."

Pablo would consider this. "No," he'd say, "it'd be you and Michael Jordan versus me."

Pablo was sixteen when I met him, another indistinguishable face in my English class of forty-five students.

I was twenty-five when I arrived as a Peace Corps Volunteer in Santa Cruz Verapaz, a town of 4,000 people. I was prepared to be alone during my entire two-year service. I figured this was the way my life was supposed to be: silent sacrifice. I wasn't, at any rate, expecting to make a friend my first night in town.

But the night after my first English class, Pablo knocked on my door. I invited him in, and he entered, looking around shyly. On a table in my dining room, he saw a copy of *Sports Illustrated* that my stepfather had sent from home. He pointed to the cover photo.

"Robert Parish," he said. "The Chief."

Pablo, it turned out, knew as much about basketball and the NBA as I did, and I was a former sportswriter.

I don't know where he got his information. *El Grafico*, the only newspaper from the capital sold daily in our town, rarely had stories about American basketball. A Mexican TV station that reached Santa Cruz showed NBA games on Saturday mornings, but the town's electricity was so unpredictable—occasionally it would be off for three or four days in a row—that I wondered how many of these games he could have seen. Pablo just seemed to know, and he was familiar not just with Robert Parish and other All-Stars; he could talk about obscure players like Chris Dudley and Jerome Kersey as if he were an NBA beat reporter.

Pablo would come to my house at night and we would draft imaginary line-ups. Pablo liked non-American players. Hakeem Olajuwon was his favorite. He liked Mark Aguirre because he'd heard that Aguirre's father was born in Mexico. Dikembe Mutombo. Manute Bol. Drazen Petrovic. Selecting our imaginary teams, he'd always draft these players first.

I didn't get it. Why would he pick Vlade Divac instead of Charles Barkley? But the longer I lived in Guatemala, the better I understood.

The American presence in Guatemala is about as subtle as a Shaquille O'Neal slam dunk. Pepsi covers entire storefronts with its logo. In Santa Cruz, the town basketball court is painted with a Coca-Cola motif, right down to the backboards. In remote villages, children wear "Ninja Turtles" tee-shirts.

We had long arguments about who was the best player in the NBA. Hakeem Olajuwon versus Michael Jordan.

Hakeem versus Patrick Ewing. Hakeem versus Magic Johnson.

Pablo stuck by his man.

Pablo and I played basketball on the court next to the cow pasture. Pablo was taller than Muggsy Bogues but shorter than Spud Webb, both of whom played in the NBA. When we first began playing, I could move him around with my body, backing him close to the basket. If I missed, I was tall enough to get the rebound. In games to twenty-one, I would beat him by nine, eleven, thirteen points.

Pablo was the first to tell me about Magic Johnson. He came over to my house one night, late.

"What is it?" I asked.

His head was bowed.

"What is it?"

He looked up. He wasn't crying, but he looked like he might need to. He said, "Magic has the AIDS virus."

We mourned together. Feeling sentimental, Pablo admitted, "Magic might be better than Hakeem."

Pablo's dream was to dunk a basketball. We calculated how many feet he would need to jump—about four.

Pablo drew up a training plan. He would jump rope two hours a day to build his leg strength. Every other day, Pablo would ask his younger brother to crouch, and he would leap over him, back and forth, for half an hour.

Two weeks later, Pablo came to my house and asked me to set up a hurdle in my courtyard. I stacked two chairs on top of each other, then another two chairs a few feet away. I placed a broom across the top chairs and measured: the broom was four feet off the ground.

"I'm going to jump it," Pablo said.

"You sure?" I asked again.

"Yes, I'm sure."

We stood there, gazing at the broom.

"You sure?" I asked.

"I'm sure."

More gazing.

Then he backed up, took a few quick steps, and jumped. His knees shot into his chest. He leapt over the broom like a frog.

"You did it!" I yelled.

"I can dunk now," he said, grinning,

The next morning, we went to the basketball court. Pablo dribbled from half court and leapt. The ball clanked off the rim. He tried it again. Same result.

"I don't understand," he said.

I didn't have the heart to admit I'd misled him: to dunk, he'd have to jump four feet without bending his knees.

As a player, though, Pablo was getting better. He could-n't dunk, but he'd learned to use his quickness to drive by me and score. He had grown stronger. I could not back into him as easily.

Also, he had developed a jump shot.

"Let's imagine," Pablo would say, "that David Robinson came to visit us."

"All right," I'd say.

"Where would he stay?"

"I don't know. At a hotel, probably."

"No," Pablo would say, "he'd stay at your house. You'd let him sleep in your bed."

"Yeah, that would be better."

"And you'd make him dinner."

"Sure."

"And at night," Pablo would say, "we'd sit around and talk about basketball."

Pablo was not my best student. He was more interested in basketball than books. But he knew how to make his teacher laugh.

When he missed a quiz, I allowed him to make it up by writing five sentences—any five sentences of his choice—in English.

He wrote:

    1. Charles Barkley sang a song in my house.

    2. I beat Patrick Ewing in slam dunk.

    3. I beat David Robinson in block.

    4. Hakeem Olajuwon is my brother.

    5. Magic and Pablo are the best friends of Mark.

Despite his interest in basketball, Pablo's best sport was soccer. He played for San Pedro Carcha, a nearby town. Pablo was known as a good play-maker. Quick dribbler. Good passer. Soccer's equivalent of a point-guard, not a power forward.

I'd seen several of Pablo's games and had watched him

make gorgeous passes, beautiful sky-touching passes that his teammates batted into the net for goals.

My last week in Guatemala as a Peace Corps Volunteer, I attended a game Pablo's team played against San Cristobal, a town nine kilometers west of Santa Cruz. The game was tied 1-1 going into the final minutes. Pablo's team had a corner kick. The crowd, about a thousand strong, was silent.

The ball soared into the air. A mass of players, including Pablo, gathered to receive it. Pablo jumped, his body shooting up like a rocket off a launcher. His timing was perfect. His head met the ball and the ball flew past the goalie.

Pablo's teammates paraded him around the field on their shoulders. People from the crowd, per custom, handed him money.

When I talked to him later, I didn't need to point out why he'd been able to jump that high. He said it himself: "It's basketball. I learned that from basketball. From trying to dunk."

We played our last game the day before I left Guatemala. We played in the evening, as a light rain—a *chipi-chipi*—fell.

He had learned to play defense. I tried to back him toward the basket, but he held his ground. I was forced to use my unreliable jump shot. I could no longer get every rebound because he'd learned to block out. And, of course, he could jump now.

I got lucky and hit two straight jumpers to pull ahead by four. But he countered with a reverse lay-up. He scored again on a long jump shot, a shot he never would have made when we first played.

The rain fell harder now. Puddles were beginning to form on the court. Pablo and I were both panting. It was getting dark; we could hardly see the basket.

"Let's quit," I said. "Let's leave it like this."

"If you want," he said.

"Yeah, let's leave it like this. A tie."

"All right," he said. "A tie. Good. Let's leave it."

We hugged each other.

"Let's imagine," Pablo said, as we walked to my house for the last time, "that you and I played against Michael Jordan. Who would win?"

"Jordan," I said.

"No," Pablo said. "We would. Believe me, we would."

Mark Brazaitis (Guatemala 1991-93) was a Volunteer and trainer in the Seed Improvement and Post-Harvest Management program. His short stories have appeared in *The Sun, Western Humanities Review, Hawaii Review* and *Beloit Fiction Journal,* and his journalism in *The Washington Post,* the *Richmond Times-Dispatch* and the *Detroit Free Press.*

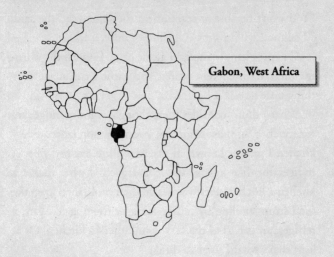

Gabon, West Africa

THE FRIDGE FACTOR
by Bonnie Black

I f you live in Equatorial Africa and you can't afford a refrigerator, you might as well kiss butter good-bye. And fresh milk and cheese and ice cream and cold drinks and last night's leftovers, too, just to name a few.

This is the latest lesson I'm learning here at my new post: how to live without a fridge, or, as one might put it in the lingua franca of this francophone Central African Country, *sans frigo*.

I can't say I wasn't warned. When my Peace Corps recruiter in New York learned I wanted to trade in my ten-year-old culinary career for a two-year stint teaching community health in Africa, he looked at me long and hard.

"You won't be able to cook or eat the same way," he said. "The food will be very . . . ahh . . . different."

"No problem," I thought at the time. I waved the warning off. "With enough onions and garlic I can make anything taste good," I bragged.

What I didn't consider then, though, was the fridge factor. Such a simple, common, everyday appliance. Every kitchen I've ever known in my whole life has had one. A refrigerator, like a sink, stove, and oven is what makes a kitchen a kitchen. First you wash, then cook, then keep the food from spoiling by refrigerating or freezing it. Why, a refrigerator is part of the very definition of a kitchen! Or at least that's what I used to think.

Now I can realize that for most of the people in the developing world, a refrigerator is a luxury item not even at the top of the list. There are four-wheel-drive cars and pickup trucks here in Lastoursville, a small town on the train line about two degrees south of the Equator. And I see glimpses of television sets blaring in mud-wattle huts as I walk by. But refrigerators? Most people here—including me—cannot afford one.

How does this affect the way people shop, cook, and eat, I wondered when I first came face to face with the problem last month. What impact does it have on their overall diet and their health? If you can't keep food from spoiling here in the rain forest, where bacteria, and all sorts of insect life thrive, what foods do you choose?

I'm in the process of finding out. This is what I've learned so far:

• **Forget leftovers.** Some claim you can leave soups and stews, covered, on the kitchen counter overnight and boil them well the next day.

• **Forget dairy products.** I've actually come to like the full-cream tinned powdered milk here; and besides, I've always wanted to cut down on my consumption of butter and ice cream anyway.

• **Forget ice cubes,** and cold drinks, and cold anything, for that matter. The sensation of having something cold in the mouth is now, at least *chez moi,* only a memory.

The trick, I've found, is to shop for fresh foods every day and cook only as much as you'll consume that day. For me this means walking about a mile to the market every morning to see what the ladies there have to offer.

"What is this, mama?" I ask an elderly African woman who has piles of leafy greens in front of her on a rough wooden table.

"Epinards," she tells me. But it doesn't look at all like the spinach I've always known and loved.

"How much?" I ask her.

"Cent francs," she says. I offer her the coin and we smile at each other as I struggle to scrunch the leaves into my net shoulder bag.

Every day I try to say a little something to each of the women there: What do you call this? How do you cook it?

For how long? What does it taste like? As well as, How are you feeling today? What is your baby's name? Where were you yesterday? I missed you!

The ladies at the market have become my friends. Their warmth, their smiles, their greetings brighten my day in a way that no refrigerator ever could.

Just the other day, one of the mamas commented on the skirt I was wearing. It was a long, blue denim A-line skirt my daughter had given me for my birthday several years ago. The old woman said, half-jokingly, half teasingly, "You could dance the tango in that skirt."

"Well, then, let's dance," I said. So she gamely got up from her wooden bench and we danced a little mock-tango—for everyone's enjoyment—right there, beside the piles of chili peppers and plantains.

Not having a fridge forces me to go to the market every day, but this is far from the hardship one might imagine. Every day I learn from these *marchandes de legumes* and enjoy experimenting with the produce I've brought back.

As soon as I get home I empty my net bag on the kitchen counter and proceed to create my "Soup du Jour"—a hearty melange of familiar and unfamiliar ingredients. Like life here in general, my soup each day is different from the one before. But the procedure I follow in making it is, like me, predictable: first I take onions and garlic . . .

Bonnie Black (Gabon 1996-98) is a Community Health Volunteer in Lastoursville, the heartland of Gabon. For many years prior to joining the Peace Corps, she was a chef and had her own catering business in New York City. She has a B.A. in Literature and Writing from Columbia University.

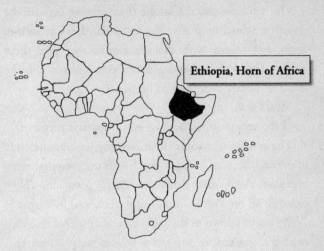

Ethiopia, Horn of Africa

SO THIS IS PARIS
by Kathleen Coskran

T he year Detroit burned, I taught English and alge-
bra in Dilla, Ethiopia. There were four of us *feren-
jis* in Dilla that year. Doug, from Michigan, saved
all the clippings from *The Christian Science Monitor* that
his mother sent him about the riots and brought them out
whenever a student asked him about his country.

He would unfold the pictures of burning buildings and
say, "This is my home."

"He reads too much," Dick said. Dick didn't have time
to read. He never missed a soccer, basketball, or volleyball
game with the students or a chance to spend an hour at
Negussie Beit, the only bar in Dilla with a refrigerator.

Our students called Claudie their mother because she stayed at school long after the sun went down to talk to them, help them with their homework, or give them advice. The day she bandaged Hamid's infected arm, he asked if she had ever been a Girl Scout.

"Yes, I was," she said.

"I thought so, miss, because you are always prepared."

The seventy-five students in 7-A, my homeroom, were impressed because I called the roll from memory every morning, Addiswork Bekele to Zeudi Memedin. They called us all the Peace Corps, but pronounced it "corpse."

We walked down to the post office after school on a clay road that sucked at our shoes in the rainy season and streaked our clothes with dust in the dry season. We passed kids shouting *"Ferenj!"* (foreigner) at us, stepped around sheep and goats crossing the main drag, stopped to admire the professional mourners in a funeral procession, paused so the water man rolling his massive barrel up the hill from the river wouldn't lose momentum. As the barrel rumbled past and the mourners took up their ululations again, and a six-year-old ran up, tagged him, and dashed back to his friends, Dick would spread his arms wide and say, "So *this* is Paris."

That year school began with a chalk shortage. One day I had used a piece of blue chalk down to only a shadow of color. Zelalem, from my sixth grade English class, asked me for the chalk after class, so I gave it to him, saying I wanted him to save it for me. Like the man and his two talents,

Zelalem gave me back twice as much chalk the next day. Somewhere he had found a grain of white chalk the same size as my spent blue piece. When I walked in the next morning, he opened his hand and proudly presented me with two precious specks of chalk for the class.

A few weeks later, in that same class, we were talking about capitalization. Each students was giving me an example of a word that is always capitalized, easy words, such as Ethiopia, Dilla, their own names. I hesitated at Nasin Shaffi, the slowest boy in the school, who was often teased by the other students. I didn't want to embarrass him again. When I asked him for a proper noun, he stood up and mumbled something.

"What?" I said.

Nasin repeated what he had said, in clear, full tones: "Dag Hammerskjold."

On St. Patrick's Day, I explained my Irish heritage to the students in 7-A and the significance of the day. Abraham, the worst troublemaker in the school, raised his hand. "We should go outside, madam, to celebrate your holiday."

"No, that's not necessary," I said, but the students were already moving toward the door.

"Yes, yes, good idea," they said.

Tsegay Mekonnen, the class monitor, stood at the door to stop them. "No," he said. "It is her holy day. We must have five minutes of silent prayer." That was not what I had in mind, but they all went back to their seats and bowed their heads.

The first time I saw Tsegay in action, he was stepping across a desk in the back of my room with a switch in his hand to hit another boy who was talking out of turn. It was my first day at Atse Dawit School.

"Hey, stop that. What do you think you're doing?" I said.

"No, madam. Is okay. He is the monitor," a student told me.

Tsegay stood against the back wall with his arms folded across his blue shirt, watching me advance on him. "I am monitor," he said when I reached him.

"Who says you are monitor?" I asked. I was familiar with the monitor system of class discipline, didn't like it, and didn't want it in my classroom.

Tsegay shrugged, but the other students confirmed that he was the class monitor. I said the monitor should be elected by the class and proceeded to explain the democratic process, the duties of the monitor (no switches allowed), the responsibilities of the students to each other, to the monitor, and to their teachers. I then took nominations from the floor. They elected Ayelu Hailu.

Because not everybody was able to start school when they were six years old, the age range of my seventh graders was twelve to twenty-two. Ayelu was a slight twelve-year-old, the smallest boy in the class, meek and overwhelmed by his sudden elevation to high office. The students snickered when I announced the election results. I insisted that they respect Ayelu, affirmed my confidence in him, and said that his word would be law regarding areas of discipline. Ayelu took a deep breath, straightened his shoulders, and strutted to the back of the room where he could keep an eye on everybody. I resumed the math lesson.

He lasted four days before quitting.

The second time around, they elected Hamid. I was pleased. Most of the students had the chiseled features, slight frame, and red-brown skin of the highland Ethiopian, but Hamid's family had emigrated from the far west. He was an imposing figure, six feet tall with very dark skin. But his service as monitor was a day shorter than Ayelu's. I didn't understand why he was unsuccessful until much later, when I heard him called "the black one" and *shankalla* (slave).

I told the students that I was furious with them for electing two successive monitors whom they refused to respect.

"Tsegay is our monitor, madam," somebody said.

And so he was. Restored to office, he became an invaluable advisor for me, an inside operator. "Bekele is not sick, madam. He have woman." Or "Kebede hates Hamid. Better move him." When I remember my class now, Tsegay's handsome face is always in the middle of the back row, his eyes roving over the rows of students. It was the end of the year before I convinced him to give up the switch.

We had electricity from six p.m. to midnight most nights. I planned lessons and graded papers when the lights were on. After midnight, I sat up with a book, reading by candlelight in the dark kitchen. I savored each word of those delicious books. I also read *Time* cover to cover every week, including the sports and business sections; I read the listings of books published on the flyleaf of Penguin library editions; I read the small print of ads in the English-language *Ethiopian Herald,* a weekly newspaper. I even read *The Fanny Farmer Cookbook* cover to cover. I knew nothing about cooking, having been raised by a mother who believed that packaged foods were the most profound scientific advance of the twentieth century.

There was no processed food in Dilla. We could dependably buy only onions, bananas, and meat. Sometimes there was cabbage and carrots. Once there was eggplant. We could also get rice, but there were insects in it. We had to dump it on the table and scrape the rice into a bowl while killing the bugs and pushing them off to the side. Salt and spices were measured into cones of old newspaper when we bought them. The egg man delivered his tiny eggs wrapped in banana leaves. When we went to Addis Ababa, we bought oatmeal, canned margarine, tuna fish, powdered milk, and tins of vegetables. The tuna and vegetables were so precious that we allowed ourselves to eat them only on special occasions. In the end, we left two cans of beets, one of green beans, and one of corn for the next Volunteers. We wrote them a long letter, introducing them to our town, our kids, and our canned vegetables.

One day, Ato Mahari and Ato Hamare, the Amhara

bankers, dropped by for tea and invited the four of us Volunteers on a picnic.

"Terrific," I said. "Do you want us to bring something?"

"Yes, of course, you women will cook, but we will hunt first. We will get partridges and two tiny antelope known as lesser kudu and have a picnic in the grand style," Ato Mahari said. Mahari and Hamare were as *ferenji* as we were in Dilla, where the people were either Sidominia or Derasse. The two of them, the four of us, plus Ato Aberra, a big man on the Coffee Board, and Ato Bekele, the school superintendent, formed the middle class of Dilla. A handful of local landowners and Negussie and Mohammed, who owned bars, were the upper class. Mahari's and Hamare's wives were shy, elegant women who didn't eat with us when we were invited to their houses. They would not be going with us on the grand picnic.

Claudie and I couldn't find a single reference to lesser kudu in *The Fanny Farmer Cookbook*. We approached Dick and Doug for help. They were sitting on their front porch with Tafesse, the third-grade teacher who lived with them. Dick had just come back from a soccer game and had a towel wrapped around his head to soak up the sweat. Doug was reading. Tafesse was smoking a cigarette.

"They expect us to cook," I said. "You have to help us."

Dick rubbed his head with the towel. Tafesse stubbed out his cigarette and grinned. Doug looked up from his book.

"You're the best cook," Claudie said to Doug. "You cook

the kudu."

"Can't," he said. "Would be insulting to Mahari and Hamare. We are guests in their country and must obey their customs."

"It is clearly woman's work," Dick said.

I said, "Come on, you guys, this is serious."

They wouldn't help us, so Claudie and I concocted something we called "cole slaw," bought bread, and gathered up some spices.

The day of the picnic, Mahari did kill two of the tiny antelope known as lesser kudu. He skinned and bled them for roasting while Hamare built the fire and Claudie and I paced nervously.

"We've got these spices," I said. But in the end Mahari roasted the delicate kudu parts himself, without the spices, and we had our grand picnic in a grove of flat-topped acacia trees under the watchful eyes of local Derasse children.

Even the most remote town in Ethiopia has one or two Italian men who married Ethiopian women after World War II and stayed on to bake bread or make pasta. In Dilla, a man named Montenari ran a small bar and the only bakery. One Friday, Dick and I stopped at his bar just before midnight. The place was empty, he was ready to close, but he still had coffee, so he poured us some, and himself some, and sat with us. He spoke no English and only a little Amharic, and we spoke no Italian, so the three of us sat there in silence, this old Italian and two young Americans, drinking espresso in the middle of Ethiopia. At midnight, the lights went out. Montenari held his hand up and shook his head, insisting that we stay. He brought candles and more coffee. We sat with him a while longer and listened to the hyenas who began their eerie calls as soon as the lights went off.

When we finally left and walked home in the dark, Dick took my hand. "Yes," he said, "Paris is like this."

I had a party for the seventy-five students in my home-room the week before we left Dilla for good. I made pop-corn and bought bananas for refreshments, but I was stumped when it came to entertainment. Music was out; our radio reception was too poor and I had no record play-er. The house was small, but I thought the kids could min-gle and talk, eat a banana, and extend the party into the yard. But they wouldn't go outside. They filled one room. I tried to engage them in conversation, but they were politely monosyllabic. I offered the popcorn, but the easy laughter and conversation from the classroom were silenced by the solemnity of the occasion. The party in my house had made them mute.

Finally, Tsegay said, "Madam, can we dance?"

"Yes, of course. But where and to what music?"

"Don't worry, miss." Tsegay issued instructions to sever-al of the students, took Addiswork's scarf, and stepped to the center of the room. Yakob found an empty patch of wall and drummed the mud plaster with the fingers and heel of his hand. Tsegay began moving in small circles in the middle of the room. The girls sang. Bekele clapped his hands in counterpoint to Yakob's drumming. Tsegay moved faster, holding the scarf taut between his hands, over his head, behind his back, then dropping an end, following it. Everybody sang, punctuating their songs with shouts and ululations.

They were of different tribes, different religions, but they knew what to do. When Tsegay finished, Addiswork took her scarf and stepped to the center of the room herself. Everybody sang and drummed as she began to move. My party was a success.

On our last day, we got up early to take the first bus to Addis Ababa. When I opened the back door in the predawn light to go to the outhouse, I discovered Tsegay, Hamid, Zeudi, Ayelu, Mulugetta, Nasin, and Zelalen waiting in the yard. Dozens of students had gathered in the dark so they wouldn't miss our departure. They hovered around our two houses as we packed. They trailed us down the dirt roads of Dilla for the last time. They insisted on carrying our things to the bus. Tsegay presented me with a basket his mother had made. "So her name will be known in your country," he said. We got on the bus and waved until we couldn't see them anymore.

The road out of Dilla is a steep climb and the bus slows to a crawl at the last switchback. There is a point where the whole town looks like a map—four parallel streets, up from the river, bisected by paths, with the school at the high end and the bus park where clumps of our kids still waved at the low end. The four of us pressed against the windows for a last look.

"So this was Paris," Dick said softly.

"This was better," I said.

Kathleen Coskran (Ethiopia 1965-67) taught English and math in Dilla, Ethiopia, and spent two years in Kenya. Her book, *The High Price of Everything,* winner of a Minnesota Book Award in 1988, includes stories set in both Ethiopia and Kenya. She recently co-edited an anthology of travel stories written by women, *Tanzania on Tuesday.* She is the principal of Lake Country Montessori School in Minneapolis.

Ukraine, Eastern Europe

To Peel Potatoes
By John P. Deever

"Life's too short to peel potatoes," a woman in my local supermarket announced, as she put a box of instant mashed potatoes into her cart. When I overheard her I nearly exploded.

After recently returning from my Peace Corps stint in Ukraine, I tend to get defensive about the potato in all its forms: sliced, scalloped, diced, chopped, grated, or julienned; then boiled, browned, french-fried, slow-fried, mashed, baked or twice-baked—with a dollop of butter or sour cream, yes, thank you.

A large proportion of my time in Ukraine was spent preparing what was, in the winter, nearly the only vegetable available. Minutes and hours added up to days spent handling potatoes. I sized up the biggest, healthiest spuds in the market and bought buckets full, then hauled them home over icy sidewalks.

Winter evenings, when it got dark at four p.m., I scrubbed my potatoes thoroughly under the icy tap—we had no hot water—until my hands were numb. Though I like the rough, sour peel and prefer potatoes skin-on, Chernobyl radiation lingered in the local soil, so we were advised to strip off the skins. I peeled and peeled, pulling the dull knife toward my thumb as Svetlana Adamovna had taught me, and brown-flecked stripe after stripe dropped off to reveal a golden tuber beneath. Finally, I sliced them into boiling water or a hot frying pan. My potatoes, my *kartopli,* sizzled and cooked through, warming up my tiny kitchen in the dormitory until the windows clouded over with steam.

Very often my Ukrainian friends and I peeled and cooked potatoes together, either in my kitchen or in Tanya's or Misha's or Luda's, all the while laughing and talking and learning from each other. Preparing potatoes became for me both a happy prelude to nourishment and, when shared with others, an interactive ritual giving wider scope and breadth to my life.

But how could I explain that feeling to the Instant Woman in a grocery store in the United States? I wanted to say, "On the contrary, life's too short for instant *anything.*"

Now, back home, I'm pressed by all the "instant" things to do. In Ukraine, accomplishing two simple objectives in one day—like successfully phoning Kiev from the post office and then finding a store with milk—satisfied me pretty well. I taught my classes, worked on other projects, and tried to stay happy and healthy along the way.

Now it takes an hour of fast driving to get to work, as opposed to twelve minutes of leisurely walking in Ukraine. I spend hours fiddling with my computer to send "instant" e-mail. Talking to three people at once during a phone call is efficient—not an accident of Soviet technology as in Ukraine. With so much time-saving, I ought to have hours and hours to peel potatoes. Somehow I don't.

What I wish I'd said to the woman in the supermarket is this: "Life's too short to be shortened by speeding it up."

But I wasn't able to formulate that thought so quickly. Instead, I went to the frozen food section and stared at the Budget Gourmet microwave dinners for awhile, eventually coming to the sad, heavy realization that the Szechuan chicken looked delicious—even if it didn't come with potatoes.

John P. Deever (Ukraine 1993-95) works at the Haas School of Business at the University of California at Berkeley. This essay won the 1996 Peace Corps Experience Award given by *RPCV Writers & Readers*.

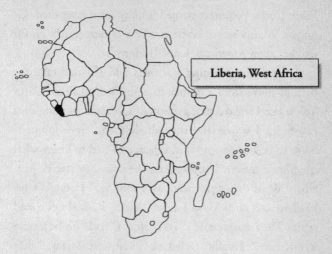

Liberia, West Africa

SAVE JOHNNY
By Paul Eagle

For the first three months I was in Africa, Liberians told me, "Save Johnny!" everywhere I went, usually as I was saying good-bye to them. Sometimes it was a group of men sharing a cup of palm wine, other times it was families gathered around a small cooking fire. I never quite knew how to respond.

I thought to myself, if I can't figure this out, how can I ever become a good Peace Corps Volunteer? How will I survive in a village by myself when I'm telling people I'll be happy to save Johnny even though I don't have a clue who Johnny is?

I thought up elaborate scenarios about how, years ago, a

Peace Corps Volunteer named Johnny must have died. Or maybe Johnny was a Liberian who was desperately ill. Or maybe, as an American, I was "Johnny."

A day before training was over, and I would take the oath to move from a trainee to a full-fledged Peace Corps Volunteer, I walked past a group of Liberians working on a rice farm. I waved and they all shouted, "Save Johnny!" Soon to be out on my own, I decided I had to know what the phrase meant. I approached them as they stared, puzzled. "What does this mean, save Johnny?" I asked. They laughed and said, "Save Johnny" again. I asked again and again. They simply said, "Take-time-o" and "To be a man is not easy." Finally it clicked: They were saying, "Safe Journey!" I was elated. The next day, when I took the oath, I thought that maybe I could make it as a Peace Corps Volunteer after all.

Now I knew what the term meant. But it would be a few months later, on my first real "journey," when I would truly come to understand this term.

It was a simple trip, about 200 miles. It was Christmas and my girlfriend, Jill, and our mutual friend, Mary, and I were going to take public transport to the Southern tip of Liberia to a town called Harper. The place held the promise of white, sandy beaches, a cool, clear ocean, and fresh seafood—a far cry from the 100 degree days in the Liberian jungle. The town also boasted a national museum and theaters with generator-driven televisions that showed movies like *Die Hard* and *The Godfather*. The only way to reach this paradise, however, was by public transport.

We met in a dusty parking lot filled with people and vans. It was Grand Central Station in the middle of the jungle. Drivers ran around, hustling people into their vans. Children cried and wailed as dust swirled in circles around the pungent smells of animals, oils, meats, and palm wine. And it was hot—hot as only a tropical rainforest can be at the peak of the dry season. The air was so thick that when smokers exhaled, their smoke could not rise or fall in the damp air; it just hung, suspended in mid-air.

In the late morning, we bought our tickets and found the van that was to take us south. We knew that the van could not leave until all the seats were filled, and since we were the first three people to buy tickets, we prepared for a long wait. Drivers and carboys ran around the packed lot, begging people to choose their van. We sat with the sun burning our foreheads.

By early evening, the van was finally full. Four large barrels of cane juice were shoved in up front, and we were jammed four to a seat in the back. Children sat on adults' laps and our luggage, live animals, and bags of rice were strapped down with rubber cords on the roof.

It was dark when we finally rattled away on the dusty dirt road, stopping to fill up with gas and attend to minor repairs on the van as we all sat patiently, crammed in our seats. The driver informed us that we would make one last stop, then would be on our way. He stopped at a cement house on a hill and went inside. We heard intense arguing in Mandingo, a tribal language. Then a woman holding a baby came running out of the house, chasing the driver. "What's going on?" I asked the man jammed against me on the left. "She is telling him that it is his baby and that he has to help pay for it. He is saying he has no money." Without warning, she reached inside the van and pulled the keys out of the ignition, then disappeared inside the house.

The tired people in the van let out a collective groan. A baby started wailing. Now soaked with sweat, I tried to picture an air-conditioned home and a cool, icy drink. For about an hour we watched the man banging on the door and the woman looking out to yell at him. Finally, an official from a makeshift courthouse in town managed to calm things down. We were finally on our way.

Once on the journey, people started falling asleep. The man sitting next to me had huge open sores on his face. I tried not to stare at him and nodded off. I woke up and found his head on my shoulder. When he woke and tried to lift his head, he couldn't. The sores had stuck to my shirt.

The cane juice began leaking and the entire van was filled with its powerful alcoholic aroma—I felt drunk from the fumes and began to get nauseous. A tethered pig urinated from the roof and two of us ended up getting soaked. The dirt road got bumpier as we traveled farther from the big town, and the potholes were so huge that many times the driver had to come to a complete stop to study them before trying to go on.

At 2:00 A.M., the van died. We were surrounded by absolute darkness, with only the sounds of the bush to let us know we were not alone. Most of the passengers got out to stretch while the driver tried to figure out what was wrong. It took me a minute to realize that, since he had no tools or flashlight, his chances of fixing the van were slim.

Just as the trip began to feel unbearable, a few of the older women, called "Old Mas," stepped off the van. So did some of the kids. The air had a chill to it, so we lit a small fire in the road and gathered around it. Some of the teenage boys began a strange dance, keeping their feet still but shaking their hips and singing. The Old Mas joined in. Then we all started laughing. We were hungry, tired, and a little cold, but we couldn't stop laughing. These rugged people had taken an impossible situation and still managed to have a good time. And then Jill, Mary, and I looked at each other and realized that the laughter washed the dust off the day. We forgot all about our bumpy, troubled transport and stopped worrying about where we would end up next.

Later a pickup came along and our driver negotiated a deal that would take all of us to Harper. So we transferred our bags and animals to the truck and climbed in. As we were leaving, the driver shouted to all of us, "Save Johnny!"

For the first time, I understood the term. It was really about the difficulties and frustrations that people suffer in the developing world dealing with things that I took for granted. It was about coping with the absurd, such as a simple day trip that ended up being a two day endeavor that left you stranded in the bush, with no food or water, stinking of alcohol, open sores stuck to your shirt, and being so tired you could hardly stand. But most of all, it was a revelation of the indomitable spirit of people who live life with joy, no matter what the situation. I smiled and, knowing that I had earned the right to use the term, shouted back, for the first time: "Save Johnny!"

Paul Eagle (Liberia 1988-90) built fish ponds and worked at a rural radio station in Belafanai, Liberia. Eagle earned a B.A. in communications and English from California State University, Chico. He lives in Baltimore with his wife, Jill, and works for a public relations firm.

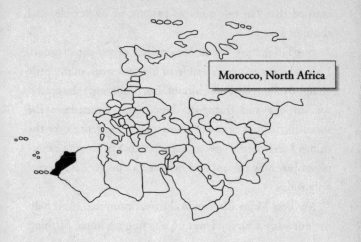

Morocco, North Africa

THE RHYTHM OF WOMEN
By Kathy Crabb

ou must be patient and flexible. You must be patient and flexible. I heard that warning so many times during the Peace Corps application process and training that it would have become a mantra if I hadn't grown so sick of it. Okay, enough already, I'm flexible! I'm patient!

Now, more than a year has passed since I was sworn in as a Peace Corps Volunteer and assigned to Morocco. My patience and flexibility have been tested in every way imaginable, from transport that shows up a day late to co-workers who value paper-pushing over useful action. I've learned that I'm not quite as patient, or as flexible, as I thought I was.

But I'm getting better. It's a matter of self-preservation. I must be patient and flexible to live and work in my little village in the High Atlas Mountains. Sometimes the road is washed out and transport doesn't run. Sometimes the social formalities of tea-drinking take precedence over the things I feel need to get accomplished. My favorite example of just how patient and flexible I've become happened only today.

My best Moroccan friend, Fadma, promised she'd help me out with a survey I was conducting on home birthing practices in the region. Since she understands my American-accented Berber better than anyone, she said she'd help interpret between me and the women I wanted to interview. Our first stop was the home of Fadma's niece, Bzza.

Bzza wasn't home when we arrived, so her mother-in-law sent a younger sister out to find her and poured Fadma and me mint tea. She told us their neighbors were having a wedding that day—we could just hear the beat of the wedding drum through the thick, warm air—but no one had come by to invite them. Fadma sipped her tea, clucked, and muttered, "Shame, shame," under her breath.

After an hour or so of tea and complaining—and still no sign of Bzza—I started to wonder if I should come back another day. I could interview Fadma herself; she had a baby about six months ago. As I was about to get up and make my excuses, Bzza burst into the room. She accepted a glass of mint tea from her mother-in-law and began clucking over the wedding invitation. I thought, this can't go on much longer. A few more clucks and I make my move.

But the conversation didn't stop—it just blasted forward, full steam ahead, growing in volume and intensity, the women's hands flying back and forth, heads thrown back in half-bemusement, half-despair as all possible aspects of the offense were examined, hashed out, and argued over.

In the end I didn't interrupt. As Bzza was pouring the fourth round of tea and I was plotting my escape for the second time in an hour, a young neighbor woman appeared in the doorway. "Come and dance!" she shouted into the room. "What are you doing?! Come to the *ahaydous!*" the wedding dance! The women sprang up with eyes on fire.

"Yallah, Dunia!" Fadma shouted, as she pulled me up by the wrist. "Let's go!" We slipped into our shoes and half-strutted, half-danced out the door and over the rocky hillside to the neighbors' house. "We'll just stay for a bit," Fadma promised me as we entered the house. "Then we'll do the interview."

I nodded. Yeah, sure. Just looking at Fadma's eyes, the way her body perked up and started moving at the mention of the *ahaydous,* I could tell we weren't going anywhere anytime soon. I calculated how many days I had left to get these interviews done, how many interviews per day that meant.

I followed Fadma's lead, circling the room, grasping each woman's hand in turn, touching children's heads, asking about everybody's health, homes, families. There were perhaps thirty women and as many children in the room. Most sat on the floor, feet tucked under them, babies tied to their backs. Some ate *taam* (thick white gruel with melted rancid butter) and others sipped steaming glasses of mint tea. One woman was a blur of glass-washing, tea-brewing, tea-pouring, tea-passing. She fed frankincense into the *mijmar* from time to time to keep the air fragrant and festive. I squeezed in against the wall, and somebody passed me a spoon. I took a few hot bites of *taam*.

A girl in the corner started up a soft drumbeat and several women, prodding and pulling others along with them, rose to form two lines facing each other. They grinned and clapped to the rhythm of the drum, pressing their shoulders against their neighbors' shoulders. One woman started a high-pitched, wailing chant that kept time with the drum. The other women joined in and the volume grew.

"A good life for the bride and groom," they chanted. "Many children . . . good health . . . prosperity . . ." One row of women began the chant and the facing line echoed back; everyone stood still, chanted, clapped, and grinned. The late-afternoon sun filtered in, winding its way between the two lines, reflecting off the swirling incense smoke, off the silver spangles on the women's bright dresses.

Slowly, then, they began to move—one woman first, a slight move right, then a small move left, her neighbors picking up her signal in domino fashion until the entire line was inching back and forth. The facing line echoed their movements, chanted in return, everyone moving just slightly; but somehow with each move the entire group shifted a little to the right.

Staying in parallel lines, they moved around each other in full circles, a little faster now, and a little faster still. Each woman in her bright spangled dress became a sparkling part of the whole beating, swishing, chanting circle, clapping, stepping, breathing the thick frankincense, looking into each other's eyes and smiling widely.

The bride was not there; these were some of the women of her extended family. The bride is seen only twice during the three-day wedding festivities—once, fully and thickly veiled, dressed from head to foot in bright red and a great deal of clanking jewelry, on the long slow parade through town. The second time, her face is uncovered but her eyes are closed as she is presented in the courtyard of her new home to members of both families. The parade and the presentation both feature an hour-long *ahaydous,* the drumming line of men and the echoing line of women. In the "co-ed" *ahaydous,* all the women but the leader keep their eyes closed, their faces down, their chants calm and quiet and even. They are shy, modest.

There was no modesty that afternoon. Someone pushed Fadma to the middle when the two lines degenerated into a ragged, pulsing circle. They tied a scarf around her hips and, with very little prodding, my best Moroccan friend shook her booty like a belly dancer in a B-movie. Fully clothed, she put on a sexier floor show than anything you could hope for at a strip bar in the United States. The rest of the room writhed and shouted, laughed and ululated, egging her on in boisterous, appreciative tones.

One octogenarian got really into it. She strutted over to the *mijmar* and flung the hem of her skirt over it to perfume her legs with frankincense smoke. She swiveled her hips back and forth for effect and pranced back to the *ahaydous,* hooting and grinning wickedly when she saw my eyes popping out.

The next time it started up, someone pulled me into the *ahaydous.* Wedged between Fadma and the risqué octogenarian, I clapped to the drumbeat and felt my heart pick up the rhythm, sensed the chants seeping into my body, kept my shoulders stiff and unmoving as my feet picked up the pattern of the slow shuffle. It could have been five minutes or five hours that we danced; it was entrancing, addicting, to become part of the rhythm and the movement of these women. Finally, with a fierce, high-pitched ululation, the drummer finished off with a flourish, a low collective shout went up, and somebody uttered a loud sigh. "Igran!" The fields. It was time to get to work, cut grass for the animals, pick potatoes for dinner.

"No, nooo, NOOOOOOOO!" someone protested.

"There's still time!" someone backed her up.

"Come on," a third chimed in, and the old frankin-censed woman hooted and rounded people up to keep dancing, keep dancing, keep dancing. A brief thought leaped through my mind about some vague job-related thing I was supposed to be doing, but I was pulled into the *ahaydous* again and found my legs moving in time with a dozen other women. The thought was gone. By the time three more calls went up to get to the fields, and three more protests beat them down, there was only half an hour of daylight left. Normally, women spend two hours each morning, and two again in the afternoon, working in the fields. There was a look of happy defiance, an unadulterat-ed joy in every body, soul, and voice that no interview could have revealed.

This was my real work, I thought. Physical health is important, but today I found out what makes these women's hearts beat, what makes their eyes shine, their skin glow, their blood flow. This was my prize for being patient, my reward for being flexible. The work will get done. But in the meantime, pass the frankincense.

Kathy Crabb (Morocco 1995-97) was a Maternal-Child Health Volunteer in M'semrir, which is located in Morocco's eastern High Atlas Mountains, where she worked with local Berber women to improve home birthing practices, prenatal care, and recognition of risk factors during pregnancy and birth. She has a B.A. in Politics from Mount Holyoke College.

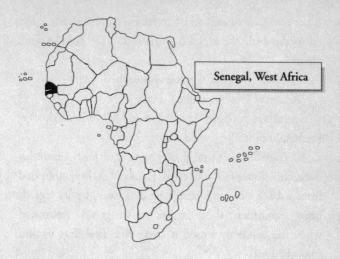

Senegal, West Africa

THE TAO OF RICE
by S. A. Snyder

S cott swerved his Honda 350 on the jungle path, nar-
rowly missing a green mamba, one of the most poisonous snakes in Africa. I clutched his waist tighter.
The dense, green tangle on both sides of us blurred as we
passed, like a cartoon tunnel carrying us from the real
world into a dream. Beige cement buildings appeared out
of nowhere among the trees and vines, as if we had discovered some lost civilization. This was the sprawling village of
Diourou in southern Senegal, near where I would be living
for the next two years.

We pulled up to Jean's house where a dozen children
and adults milled about. Scott had taught Jean how to

plant mango seedlings and start his own orchard. He wanted to show me the orchard to give me a feel for the work ahead.

"*Kasumay,*" they said as we approached. Peace.

"*Kasumay keb,*" we replied. Peace only.

Scott introduced us. I panicked and fell back on sketchy French, hoping they could understand.

Jean walked us through a maze of corridors inside his dark, cool house to the kitchen. His mother, Inay, appeared from a back doorway, clutching a chicken by its legs. It hung motionless, then flapped its wings and squawked when she carelessly tossed it aside. She smiled at us and squawked too.

"*Kasumay!*"

"*Kasumay keb,*" we replied. Jean and Scott told Inay who I was and what my mission in Senegal was. She smiled and laughed, but threw me suspicious glances. Then Jean quietly conferred with Inay, who listened intently before knitting her brows and screeching an angry reply. Scott looked at me. My eyes begged for a translation.

Several minutes of negotiation passed between Inay and Jean. Scott gave me a quick translation.

"He wants to show you the vault," Scott said, motioning to a large box suspended from the ceiling. "It's where they keep the rice." Inay shook her head, pointed to me, and made an angry remark to Jean. "She doesn't want you to see it," Scott said. Jean's voice grew more demanding, while Inay held her ground. "She doesn't think you're

Diola," Scott said.

"I'm not," I said, wanting to leave.

"You will be soon." Scott ribbed me with his elbow. "Use your Diola name."

Inay turned to me, sighed, and said, *"Kasumay."*

"Kasumay keb," I said, shrugging my shoulders. Hadn't we already been through this? She looked at Jean, then turned back to me.

"Kares'I bu?" she asked.

Quick, what was my Diola name? *"Saly,"* I said, gaining a bit of confidence. She pressed on.

"Kasaaf'I bu?" I had my Diola surname on my tongue.

"Mane," I said, now rising to the challenge.

"Au bay?" Inay threw her head back, confident I would fail. Should I say, "America," or give her the name of my future Diola village? I hesitated, and she smiled, certain she had me.

"Dana," I replied. Quickly she retorted, *"Kata sindo'ay?"*

"Kooku bo," I answered. My people are there; they are fine.

Inay squealed and clasped her hands together. She turned to Scott, waving her arms and chattering in Diola I didn't understand. He laughed. Inay grabbed my hand and led me to the ladder that rose into the sacred vault. I suddenly took an interest in rice. We crouched side by side in the blackness of the vault. Jean brought up a lantern. Hessian bags, enough to sustain a small family through a drought year, were revealed in its glow. Inay stroked one of the plump bags, speaking to me with care now.

She plucked a small handful of spilled grains from the floor and displayed them in her palm. She separated one, rubbed it between her thumb and finger, and talked about the rice. I began to see its significance, even though I couldn't understand her words.

"Help me, Scott. I need to understand," I said.

Inay pounded her empty fist on her palm.

"She says they have to beat it," Scott yelled up to me. Inay shook an invisible object in her hands.

"Then they sift out the chaff," Scott continued. Inay pummeled her palm again.

"Then they pound it a second time," Scott said. Inay opened her palm, the rice grains wet from moisture. She flicked a few grains off, and they stuck to one of the bags.

"The girls pick out the rest of the chaff, then it's pretty much ready," Scott's voice trailed up the ladder.

Inay showed me her worn, wrinkled hands and cradled one inside the other. Her voice was soft now, tired. She took my right hand and turned my palm upward. She scooped up another small handful of rice from the floor and placed the grains in my hand.

"Un cadeau," she said in French. A gift.

Scott drove a little slower on our way to Jean's orchard. The countryside opened up a bit where farmers had cleared native forest to plant fruit trees.

"You should feel honored," Scott yelled over the engine's rattle. "It's not often they trust us like that."

We rolled to a stop just outside a fenced enclosure.

Inside were hundreds of knee-high mango trees. Scott steadied the bike while I swung off.

"That was like showing you the family jewels," he said. "She wouldn't have done that if she didn't think you were going to make a good Diola."

We wandered among the four-year-old mango seedlings. For three months I had planted and cared for several hundred tree seedlings in my own makeshift nursery. I appreciated the sweat of digging holes; the excitement of measuring your trees' growth every day; the disappointment of coming to water them in the morning and finding brown, curled leaves and drooping stems. I loved the fact that Diolas wouldn't cut down the giant fromagier trees with their smooth webbed bases, because the trees harbored evil spirits that would kill your chickens or make your family sick. I marveled at these people who found a use for every part of a tree—food, medicine, clothing—without cutting it down. Trees I understood. Rice I was just beginning to learn about.

S. A. Snyder (Senegal 1990) was a forestry trainee in Thies, Senegal. Snyder has degrees in Forestry, Wildlife Biology, and Journalism from the University of Montana. She lives in Missoula, Montana.

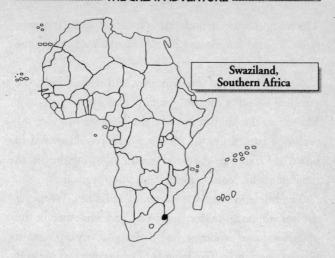

Swaziland,
Southern Africa

WOOD-LOOKING
by Sam Birchall

It was 4:30 a.m. and I was sitting at the "bus station," which is, in fact, a large boulder at the side of the dirt road about a five-minute walk from my house. The moon was bright enough for me to write in my notebook, and the sun was still an hour from rising. I knew that I was at the correct boulder because it was the one that says "Jesus is Coming" on the side. When I first saw the message glowing dimly in the moonlight, I wondered if He would get here before the bus, and if so, how much would He charge for a lift to Manzini. There was not a soul in sight, and only the crowing of a rooster drowned out the whispers of the wind in a lone pine tree across the road.

The boulder was uncomfortable to sit on while trying to write. I could see about a mile down the road, where the bus would be coming from.

Suddenly, I heard voices nearby, and then, faintly, the growling sound of the bus, grinding through the gears as it labored up the hill just out of sight. I saw its two glowing eyes as it crested the hill. About fifteen people arrived to board it. I could see the cloud of dust following the bus in the moonlight, looking like a long, sinuous snake.

The ride into town was strenuous and dusty. Whenever the bus stopped, the dust caught up and whooshed in the open windows. Someone had tied a goat on top, and it bleated constantly. The large lady sitting next to me was clutching a chicken in a plastic grocery bag with its head sticking out. Every once in a while it would cluck loudly and struggle to escape the bag, flapping and squawking for a minute before it settled down. The woman paid no attention to it.

In Mbabane, I got my pay—the modest living allowance that all Peace Corps Volunteers receive—did some quick shopping, and arrived at the Peace Corps office at about 9:45 a.m. The transport driver was waiting. It was Bongmusa, the same one who had taken me out to my school when I first arrived in Swaziland. We loaded up and drove to Piggs Peak and on to Mondi Timber. I had written to the manager of Mondi Timber explaining that it was difficult to teach woodworking without wood and asking if he could donate some scraps.

The drive from Mbabane to Piggs Peak was about sixty kilometers. It was a beautifully scenic route. I had started the day at sea level, in a scrub desert climate, and traveled through the middle veld, where the fruit trees and major grain crops were grown, and three hours later I was at 3,500 feet above sea level, driving through towering eucalyptus and pine forests. It was much cooler in the mountains, and the streams were clear, fast, tumbling water, instead of the muddy and sluggish trickles that I was used to.

Mondi Timber was a huge lumber operation with a large sawmill. I found the yard manager and followed him to his office. I introduced myself and explained what I needed. He took me back to the yard and pointed out some piles of rough-sawn, slightly weather-beaten planks, and told me to take what I wanted. I thanked him warmly.

I got the driver to bring the truck around, and we started loading the planks, stacking them neatly in the bed. When the load reached the level of the sides, I was ready to call a halt. Bongmusa disagreed. He explained that since the Peace Corps would let me have the truck only once during the school year, I should get as much lumber as I could. We went back to stacking wood. Bongmusa poked some one-by-twelve planks into the sides, standing on end, and before long, the wood was about a foot higher than the cab. The truck was squatting down in back from the weight of the wood. Finally, Bongmuse was satisfied. We tied the load down as securely as we could. I have never seen a truck so overloaded. I asked Bongmusa if he was sure that we would make it all the way to Elulakeni without breaking down. He assured me that he had carried heavier loads.

As we rolled slowly out the gate of the lumberyard, I felt like Jed Clampett of the *Beverly Hillbillies*. So strong was the feeling that I broke into the theme song. "Well, let me tell y'all a story 'bout a man named Jed, a poor mountaineer, barely kep' his fam'ly fed . . ."

Bongmusa listened carefully. When I finished, he asked, "Is that a traditional song in America, Sam?"

"Yes, Bongmusa, it is a song that we sing when we have a load that is very large on our trucks," I replied. How else was I going to explain it?

"Was the man named Jed your King? And do your mountains have ears?" He was seriously trying to make sense of the song.

I spent half an hour trying to explain the premise of the *Beverly Hillbillies* show. It didn't translate well between our cultures.

Only the first hundred or so miles back to school were on a paved road. As soon as we hit dirt road some of the wood slid off the truck. We stopped and reloaded it and retied it. We did this six times before we reached the school. The rough road made the overloaded truck seem to waddle like a duck. More than once, I thought that we would tip over completely. There was no electricity at Elulakeni, so we unloaded the lumber in darkness, throwing it through the open back door of my woodworking shop, into a huge jumble.

I was extremely happy to have it. There was more than enough wood for all my classes for the next year or more. Some of the wood was going to make benches for my classroom so the boys would have the luxury of sitting.

What a useful thing wood is for a woodworking class. But so far I only had the means to teach "wood-*looking*." Now all I needed was some tools.

Sam Birchall (Swaziland 1991-93) was a Woodworking and Technical Drawing teacher in Elulakeni, in the Kingdom of Swaziland. He has a B.A. in Economics and Management from Wilmington College, Ohio, and lives now in Austin, Texas.

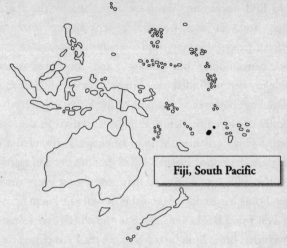

Fiji, South Pacific

LIVING BY THE BOOK
by Donna Gessell

O n Fiji, books were scarce in our village, Naqelewai. All material possessions were scarce because of the village's remote location. Despite the two-day journey involving dusty bus rides and a muddy Land Rover trek, I brought in five cartons of books, many of them Peace Corps issues with titles like, *Small Business Projects for Rural Villages* and *Raising Chickens in the Bush*. I also tucked in books for comfort like *The Joy of Cooking, The Tao te Ching,* and *War and Peace*. Later I picked up junk, mystery, and romance novels from other Peace Corps Volunteers and from bookstores in the capital. During my two years in Naqelewai, I read everything I could find, including *Newsweek,* furnished by the Peace Corps, and *National Geographic,* sent by my parents. *National Geographic* may seem a strange choice, given my exotic surroundings, but reading it and piling past issues beside my bed reminded me of my childhood and home.

Reading, however, is not part of the Fijian culture, historically or currently. Before Europeans arrived in the last century, Fijian was not a written language. Early missionaries soon developed English-Fijian dictionaries and translated the Bible into Fijian, so that now almost every rural Fijian home has a copy of the Bible as well as a Fijian hymnal. Few other books find space in the clutter-free house. Newspapers brought in by travelers are read and passed on, then used for a variety of non-literary purposes, including stencil designs for decoration under the tin cans that hold house plants, and as crumpled balls used in place of tissue in outdoor toilets. Few rural Fijians read for pleasure, other than the occasional letter from family, although elementary education is almost universal.

Pleasure reading is made difficult because of the lack of electricity. With little artificial light, people in Naqelewai get up with the sun and do most of their activities during daylight. After dark, dinner is served by the light of kerosene lanterns. Conversation follows, sometimes late into the evening, lit by that same dim light.

Despite my investment in a propane lantern, the inevitable eyestrain cut short my periods of night reading. I sometimes read during the after lunch rest, but reading at other times of the day, when everyone else was working, put me at risk of being thought strange. Wanting to fit in, I tried to limit my appetite for the written word to leisure time.

Sundays, always a favorite day for me to relax with a good book, was not conducive to reading. The day was dedicated to visiting—that is, sitting around and talking for what seemed interminable hours until I finally learned to discuss issues, gossip, and tell jokes in Fijian. During those visits, I learned invaluable information about village life that aided my work, but I often found myself longing to be tucked away with a book.

I enjoyed the intimacy of community discussion, but I missed the intimacy of reading and identifying with fictional characters. My longing made me question my basic assumptions. Which was healthier: participating in community talk or solitary reading?

At times my solitary reading habits became occasion for community talk: "There's Daiana. She always has a book in her hand." In fact, one afternoon when my next-door neighbor came by and found me reading, she voiced her curiosity. She asked if all Americans read as much as I did, if Americans ever neglected their household and family duties to read, and if Americans ever missed work to read a good book. Her questions reminded me of the list of questions posed to suspected alcoholics.

Indeed, other incidents reaffirmed my suspicions that I was a book junkie. One day as I was preparing dinner, a friend came by with out-of-town relatives. After the usual introductions ("Here's our Peace Corps—Daiana"), the woman ventured to demonstrate just how exotic a specimen a "Peace Corps" was. "Look at her," she said, pointing out the cookbook lying open at my side. "She does everything by a book. She even uses one to cook."

Indeed, I began to realize just how much I did "by the book," or "books," to be more precise. For instance, if I wanted to work with the village nurse on a nutrition education project, I consulted the *Lik-Lik Book* for information from projects conducted by village development workers in Papua New Guinea. I looked up food information and recipes in the Fijian Women's Club *Kakana Vinaka* and Susan Parker's *Fijian Cookbook*. I consulted food leaflets my Peace Corps Volunteer friend Sikandra Spain was developing for the South Pacific Commission. I used Peace Corps manuals to get ideas for poster presentations. And it wasn't just Peace Corps projects that sent me to books. I read for pleasure, falling asleep and waking up with books.

It is no wonder that, when my house accidentally caught fire, the first items the Fijians rushed to save were the books. They knew what was important to me. Despite the almost irreplaceable pieces of Fijian *tapa* cloth and a war club hanging in the house, they reached for my books first. They recognized my values even though they did not share them.

It is ironic that, of all my projects in Naqelewai, the primary school library is my lasting legacy. When the school was being rebuilt, the headmaster requested a library. He set aside the space in the building, and I contacted agencies that collect and distribute new and used books. Ten chests of books arrived, and some fifth-and sixth-graders helped sort and process the books. When the new building was finished, the headmaster declared the library the most important part of the new school, and he predicted a long future of reading for his students.

Donna Gessell (Fiji 1979-82) was a community development Volunteer in Naqelewai, Fiji, where she worked with five villages on development projects, and in Suva, Fiji, where she helped train women community leaders from across the Pacific at the Community Education Training Center of the South Pacific Commission. Gessell has a Doctorate in English Literature from Case Western Reserve University and is Assistant Professor of English at North Georgia State University.

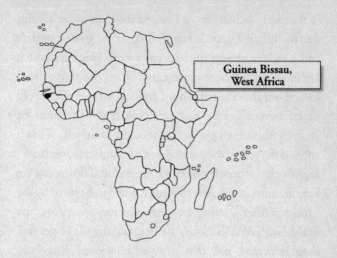

Guinea Bissau,
West Africa

MY SIDE VS. THEIR SIDE
by Roz Wollmering

My Side

I entered the school brimming with ideas, innovative teaching methods, and the desire to have an effect. It was the first day of school in Guinea-Bissau, the tiny West African country where I had been assigned as an English teacher with the Peace Corps. After completing an exhausting and demanding twelve weeks of training in language as well as cross-cultural and technical skills, I felt more than adequately prepared for the challenge of teaching in a poor school system designed on a colonial model.

Inside the building, I noticed a strange absence of noise. A few students wearing white school jackets rambled about in the dimly-lit hallway. As I neared the stairs to the administrative office, I heard a mango drop to the ground outside and a sudden chorus of children's voices. Hoping to catch a glimpse of the fastest one carrying off the ripe prize, I looked out into the schoolyard and saw instead piles of old desks, broken bricks, and tree branches. They must be cleaning the school grounds, I thought to myself. When I entered the office, the principal and his assistant were looking at a class schedule posted on the wall and discussing the large number of teachers that still needed to be hired by the Ministry. After greeting me warmly by inquiring about my health, my family back in America, and my life in general, they informed me that my teaching load had been increased by eight hours since the previous week. "No problem," I responded, "I love to teach."

I glanced at my watch, excused myself, and hurried to my first class, which was located a short distance behind the main building. Three lines of classrooms were arranged in rows, like military barracks. Since it was the first day of classes, I hopped on my bicycle and coasted right up to the door of classroom number nineteen—my classroom. "Always wiser to be punctual and prepared than tardy and unequipped," I told myself. Two students were sitting inside the classroom, playing cards, when I entered. I looked at the official enrollment number of forty-seven and asked earnestly, "Where are the other students?" The card players faltered a bit and then mumbled, "They'll come, by and by."

"Well, let's begin without them," I suggested, with a disapproving stare at the cards. They shrugged their shoulders and offered to go and find the students. It certainly didn't seem reasonable to me to teach two students and then have to teach the same material again when the others showed up. Be flexible, I reminded myself, and so I agreed.

One week later, there were twenty-six students outside my classroom, waiting for the rest of their classmates to appear "by and by." They refused to enter until all the enrolled students had showed up. I noticed that not only were students absent, but teachers as well. Meanwhile, the principal and his assistant were still discussing the schedule on the wall, moving multi-colored pins, and deliberating about how best to resolve the shortage of teachers. That morning I had stopped by the administrative office again just to make sure that I had understood correctly the radio announcement made by the Minister of Education the previous evening. I thought that he had announced that classes were in session and was quite relieved when the principal verified my assessment. He then asked me to teach an additional two hours a week. Lacking the experience to rebut his statement that "when there's a lack of teachers, we all need to pitch in a few extra hours," I nodded in consent. Considering that I wasn't actually teaching any students at the time, two extra hours didn't seem much of a burden, and I left, feeling only a mild premonition that I might regret it later.

By the end of the third week, I had managed to convince, cajole, and beg my students to enter the classroom. What other teachers did was their decision, I figured, but as for me, I was itching to do something other than wait on shore like a seafarer's wife. Once the students had entered, I discovered to my amazement that I couldn't get them to quiet down. Ignoring my requests to pay attention, they continued to socialize. Daisy painted her nails and chatted with Aminata about the new discotheque called "Temptation" that had just opened across from the mosque. Bebe took Nanda's notebook and wouldn't return it. Fatu gave me the peace sign and went outside to urinate. A few others followed. Students wandered in late with irrelevant excuses like, "It's hot," or, "I'm tired." Nelson and Marcelino held competitive "jive" talks while their classmates gathered around encouraging first one and then the other. Other students, whose teachers were absent, hung around the open windows, throwing crumpled-up balls of paper to their friends. Others simply came to stare at me, a white woman who rode a bicycle to school. They shoved up against the outside wall, clambered over each other's backs, and stuck their heads in for a peek, yelling, "White woman, white woman, there she is!" The next day, still more "window students" appeared to torment me. Such behavior continued daily and eventually I began to yell at them—"Get away from the windows!"—and resorted to pushing them out of viewing range. After a month at my new post, I reigned over thirty hours a week of complete disorder in a pseudo-classroom kingdom. This is madness, I thought.

For the next month, I devoted the first twenty minutes of class solely to establishing peace and quiet. I was determined. I did this with gentle coaxes at first, but gradually evolved to using threats ("I'll call the school disciplinarian!") and offering sweet enticement ("If you're good, I'll let you out early!"). Late students were not allowed to enter, regardless of their excuses. It seemed the only way to control the chaos. Once I had my students' attention, I made them copy page after page of notes from the blackboard into their notebooks. I wanted to inundate their minds with grammar rules and vocabulary lists so they wouldn't have time to talk. Other times, I made them repeat sentences in unison as if they were Berlitz parrots. Audio-lingual theorists suggest that language is acquired through repetition of recurring patterns, a proposition effectively demonstrated when I overheard my students mimicking me: "Be quiet! Go sit down!"

When the drudgery of memorization and repetition began to bore even me, I resorted to playing Bingo, Simon Says, or Do the Hokey-Pokey. I went to elaborate lengths to make nifty prizes for positive reinforcement and spent countless hours designing educational posters for the walls. For a time, I concentrated on visual stimulation and drama to reinforce right-brain learning, but the posters disappeared overnight and the drama idea erupted one day during a production of a local folk tale: my fellow teachers disapproved of thrashing crocodiles, bellowing hippos, and trumpeting elephants during school hours. The students whined like eight-year-olds and threw verbal tantrums when they could no longer perform or play games. I rather enjoyed their drama productions myself, and I figured they were reviewing English grammar and vocabulary by playing the games. But deep inside of me arose a persistent, nagging voice: "Surely you can do more than baby-sit."

Gradually, as discipline turned my classroom into a virtual boot camp, my classes began to develop a catatonic personality. Somber students stared back at me or out into space. Apathy replaced the boisterous noise I had grown accustomed to fighting. They refused to open their notebooks until I'd repeated the request three times. Orders and instructions mollified them, sure enough, but now they didn't seem to have opinions, concerns, or even interests. Some simply put their heads down and slept. Sit and listen they did, but participate and discuss and collaborate they didn't. Their passive resistance soon infuriated me, and I yelled in frustration at them, "I am here to help you. Don't you understand that?" They stared at me in dazed disbelief. "What do you want?" I implored them with open hands: "Do you want me to entertain you? To treat you like military recruits? To punish you?" They shrugged their shoulders and sighed, "Teacher, we are pitiful. That's life." "Go," I told them. "Go home. Get out." They refused, of course.

Against my better judgment, I finally called in the

school disciplinarian. The moment he arrived, every single student in the classroom jumped up to attention. They greeted him in perfect unison with a resounding, "Good morning, Mr. Disciplinarian." When he ordered them to sit down, an immaculate silence spread throughout the classroom. I was astounded. They looked so serene and innocent as they waited attentively for his words. Their perfect composure made them look like harmless babes, and I began to imagine that they would convince him of their purity and that I was the evil abuser. I began to wonder, in fact, if this wasn't perhaps partially true.

The disciplinarian picked out several students who were not wearing school jackets, and a few who were but had not buttoned the top button. He accused them of intentionally belittling their American teacher and expelled them for two weeks. He then read a list of seven students' names. Since these students had registered for classes but had not yet paid their school fees, he expelled them for the year, adding an insult as they crept out of the classroom. He then turned to me and said, "If any of these students ever give you a problem, no matter how small, you tell me, and I will expel the entire class for the entire year. Not one of them will pass, and they will all have to repeat the year." As I struggled to come up with a suitable response, he turned back to the students, held up one finger, and challenged them, "Just one of you try it. Just one, and I'll whip your ass." And then he left. I stood in horrified shock and embarrassment. I had just lost thirteen students. The students said nothing. They stared at me and waited to see what I would do next. I felt angry and stupid and offered a feeble apology. I fumed all the way home.

That night I dreaded going back to the classroom the next morning. I thought about ending my Peace Corps service and going home. I was sure I could find a justifiable excuse for a graceful exit. It was now the third month of teaching and quarterly grades were due in ten days. All I had managed to teach were two review units. Two review units! Most of these students couldn't even meet the standards of the previous year's curriculum! How did they manage to pass? I was tempted to flunk them all myself this time around, but what would that accomplish? I looked in dismay at the stack of twenty-five lesson plans I had diligently prepared during the late night hours of the past two months and realized that I would never use them.

So I switched strategies. That night I drew up a "No More" list. No more colorful visual aids to catch their attention. No more fancy vocabulary and grammar handouts. No more games. No more prizes. And no more school disciplinarian to resolve crises.

My next unit began with the following dialogue:

Teacher:	I am angry. I cannot teach because you do not respect me.
Students:	No, no, Teacher. Please, Teacher, please.
Teacher:	I don't want to teach you. I'm leaving.

Students:	No, Teacher, no. Please, Teacher. You see, you don't understand our situation.
Teacher:	Well, tell me, just what is your "situation?"

This time the dialogue was theirs to complete and resolve.

Their Side

It was Tino and Mando who came and told us that a skinny, white woman had jumped off a bicycle, run into our classroom, and tried to teach them English that morning. Tino and Mando weren't even in our class. They were just sitting there waiting to use the soccer field when she rushed in like the rains. They weren't sure what to say because she looked so strange. Her hair was all falling down, and she wore a dress that looked like an old faded bed covering that one might have bought from a Mauritanian vendor in the used clothing market. We all walked over to Nito's house and found a few more of our classmates sitting out back drinking frothy tea. We decided, even though school hadn't really started yet, that we'd go the next day to see what this new American teacher looked like. Tino and Mando assured us that she was as ugly as a newly hatched, greedy-eyed vulture.

We knew that almost no one would be at school yet. Most students were still on the farms, finishing the harvest, and others were still trying to register and pay their fees. The Ministry had changed the admission rules again. All registrations completed at the end of the last year were now declared invalid, and so we had to wait in line, get new photographs, show our papers, and pay fees all over again—either that, or pay some official to put our names on the list, which actually was much easier than completing the registration process. We listened to the radio broadcasts of the Minister, reminding parents about the importance of school. Everybody knew he sent his children to the private Portuguese School.

As it turned out, we agreed to enter the classroom just when everyone else did. We always say: "Cross the river in a crowd and the crocodile won't eat you." From that first day, she never demanded our respect. She didn't seem to care if we wore our school jackets or not. She didn't write the teaching summary on the board like our other teachers, and she was always in the classroom before the bell rang. That meant we could never stand up and honor her entrance. She should have known not to enter until after the bell rang. And she never took roll call first, as she should have, and so we continued talking and doing our homework. Of course, by this time, other students had heard about our white woman teacher and were coming by to look at her and watch our class. We couldn't resist joining in the fun. At times, we believed she was serious, for example, when she told the students outside class to leave. But where were they supposed to go? The area in front of her classroom was the designated student recreation area. Instead of ignoring them and us, she berated them with gestures and scolded us in Portuguese. Her Portuguese wasn't bad, but it sounded so funny when she said, "Spoiled brats!" that you just had to laugh. We laughed even harder every time she said "Peace Corps" because in our Kriolu language, "Peace Corps" sounds like "body of fish." We called her the "fish-body teacher" after that.

Classes were interesting because they were unpredictable. She kept switching her methods, and we were never sure what to expect next. For a while she insisted that the mind equips itself and a teacher must not interfere in the process. She called that, "silent way." After the "silent way" came "Total Physical Response." We gave actions to everything and pretended to be desks, pencils, and other classroom articles. We twisted our bodies around and played "What Am I?" Then we role-played imaginary dialogues between, for example, two books fighting to get into a book bag at the same time. One day she taught us the song, "In the Jungle." We loved that song. No, you couldn't really call her a consistent person, but we all have our little ways. Even so, "a cracked calabash can still be mended." Obviously, she cared about us because she worked so hard to prepare class. Most of our teachers were so busy at home or working a second or third job that they often missed class, and when they did show up, they had never prepared anything. It's true that we've already learned more English this quarter than we learned all last year.

We always wanted to do more activities and play new games, but she thought we needed to write. Because we didn't have books, she kept demanding that we copy information down on paper. But Guineans are oral people. We learn by talking; we make discoveries by sharing our experiences; and we help others by listening and contributing to conversations. Our history is a collective memory, and we are continually passing our knowledge on to others in our speech. She wanted us to raise our hands, one by one, and then talk individually. To us that seemed wrong.

She confused us even more by saying pointless things with vigor—"Wake up! Discover yourselves!"—or asking questions that had no obvious answers: "Why are you here?" or "What are you going to do?" Then she'd wait with such an intent expression on her face that we'd say almost anything to try to please her. We always enjoyed her facial expressions because they foretold what was to follow— anger, joy, disappointment, praise, or contentment. She really should have learned by then how to hide or show her feelings to suit her purpose more effectively, but she didn't seem to care. In some ways, she was just like a child.

We just didn't understand why it was our thinking that needed to change, and never hers. She wore a "bad eye" charm around her neck, so we thought she was superstitious, but when we asked her, she said she wore it to show respect for our culture. We asked her if that was why foreigners always wanted to buy our ritual masks and initiation staffs, but she didn't answer. She told us we didn't need World Bank handouts and International Monetary Fund debts. What we needed, she said, was to learn how to raise fish. Was she crazy? We need computers, not fish! Balanta women always know where to find fish. "Teacher," we told her, "you will come and go, but we stay here." How could she understand our culture? She had only seen the rains fall once.

After a while, the novelty wore off, and we got tired of even a white woman's ways. It's hard—waking up at day-break, doing morning chores, and then going to school for five hours without eating breakfast. Her class was during the last hour, and we were as hungry as wild animals by that time. Some of us lived far from school, and if our step-uncle or older cousin-brother told us to go to the market before school, we had no choice. We were forced to run to her class with only a bellyful of worms because we knew she wouldn't listen to our misfortunes even if we arrived two minutes late. It's true! In America, time is money, but here time is different. Time is just now, nothing more.

It wasn't only that we had responsibilities at home that came before school—sometimes we were sick. If we had malaria, we'd put our heads down and sleep. And if we had "runny belly," we'd just run out of class when the cramping started. The dry season was so hot that we faded away like the songs of morning birds. One day she yelled at us. We admit, we weren't cooperating, but people are like that. We forgive each other and just go on. "That's life," we'd tell her, "a log, as long as it stays in the water, will never become a crocodile." Many things we just accepted as nat-ural, but she considered such an attitude "fatalistic."

Finally, she called the school disciplinarian on us. She should have done that much earlier, in our opinion. We played our roles by allowing him to throw out a few students, because we all knew they'd be back as soon as he got some cashew-wine money from them. Anyway, that's the right of elders in our culture, and we're taught in the bush to live by the established rules. We didn't understand why she apologized after he left, and we couldn't believe it when she undermined his authority by apologizing for his "poisonous pedagogy," as she called it. Like a Guinean woman, she certainly had courage.

Today, she did something different again. She came in and wrote a dialogue on the board. She asked questions about the dialogue that made us disagree. We had a lively discussion in English and then got into our groups and began designing some solutions for the problem presented in the dialogue. We always say, "When the ants unite their mouths, they can carry an elephant."

We know she'll stay, too. We saw it in her eyes.

Roz Wollmering (Guinea-Bissau 1990-92) has an M.A. in Chinese from the University of Minnesota and a B.A. in Spanish and Biology from Saint Cloud State University, Minnesota. A former Associate Peace Corps Director in the Baltics, she works in the Peace Corps Office of Placement in Washington, D.C.

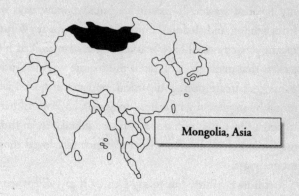

Mongolia, Asia

COLD MORNINGS
by Matthew Heller

Our family always lived where we needed a snow shovel. I remember one snowstorm in particular when I was nine. My best friend, Bobby Frost, and I shoveled our entire driveway ourselves, which is no small feat for nine year-olds. When we were done, my father was waiting in the kitchen to reward us with grilled cheese sandwiches, tomato soup, and a silver dollar for the work we had done. Dipping my grilled cheese into the steaming tomato soup (in my opinion, truly the best way to eat the two together), I am sure I was oblivious to how lucky I was; how Norman Rockwell-beautiful shoveling a driveway can be.

Because I grew up in New England, winter was always my favorite season. It meant ice hockey, snow days off from school, and sledding until dinner was ready. Winter meant scratchy wool hats, scarves that always choked me, jackets that made me look like a mini-sumo wrestler, snow pants that made peeing an ordeal, and moon boots. My moon boots were my favorite. I may even have worn them to bed a few times, afraid someone would take them from me while I slept. I loved winter as much as I loved those moon boots.

I still love winter, but to say I enjoy it as I did when I was nine years old would be a lie. I've been a Peace Corps Volunteer in Mongolia for eighteen months now and I live in a *ger,* a tent with a small wood stove in the center. It is strong and practical, the perfect domicile for a nomadic herder living on the Asian steppe. It packs up in about half an hour. I, however, am not a herder, but an English teacher in a small secondary school in rural Mongolia. *Ger* life is not easy. It makes twenty year-olds look thirty-five. It makes your soul hard.

Mongolians are very proud of their history and traditions. Once, while sitting on the train going from Ulaanbaatar, the capital of Mongolia, to my own town, Bor-Undur, a Mongolian pointed to his arm and said, "In here is the blood of Genghis Khan. Beware." Really, there is no argument to that statement. I responded, "Yes, older brother (a respectful title addressed to elders), your country is beautiful. Mongolians are lucky people."

Unfortunately, many Mongolians are big vodka drinkers, and this very drunk herder was on his way home from selling cashmere wool and meat in the city. He had been successful in his business, celebrating, and he wanted to teach me the custom of taking the traditional three shots of vodka that new acquaintances must drink. His shots were too big for me, and I only wanted to taste the vodka, not help him finish the bottle. That's when Genghis' blood came into the conversation. I drank the three shots. Herders are tough people. They don't wear moon boots.

Maybe if I had been born here and lived in a *ger* all my life I would be tough too. But I wasn't, and I'm not. I can trace no lineage to the man who was once the world's most powerful ruler, but I am blessed. I am blessed with the gift of a Peace Corps/Mongolia standard issue sleeping bag rated to -30 degrees. When combined with another sleeping bag of my own and some wool blankets, I am completely protected from the cold that invades my *ger* every night when the fire goes out.

When it's time to wake up and start my day, the first thing I do is build a fire. In the quiet darkness of morning, huddling next to my stove and sipping hot coffee, I listen to the Voice of America on my shortwave radio and remind myself who I am, where I'm from, and what I'm doing. I'm a young Volunteer spending eight hours a day with Mongolians, building a greenhouse with the other teachers in my school so there will be more vegetables in our town. Along with many other things, I'm learning how they live.

In the steppe there is very little snow, only biting wind and dust. It gets as cold as -50 degrees, not counting the wind chill factor. If I leave leftover tea in a mug, it will freeze solid by morning. I've broken three mugs that way. When it is this cold I sometimes ask myself, "How valuable is the contribution I'm making? And is it really worth being this cold?"

For eighteen months now I've been waking up and thinking, yes, it is. I love working with Mongolians, but the time of day I look forward to most is building my morning fire. It is my time of epiphany. As I feel the warmth that my own hands created, a fire that pushes back the cold and the dark, replacing them with warmth and light, I know I will live another day. Such an experience defines what it means to be a Peace Corps Volunteer.

We all build fires in one way or other, and the warmth we create is as good as eating grilled cheese sandwiches and tomato soup on a winter day when you're only nine years old. Being a Volunteer in Mongolia and having the opportunity to live in a *ger* may mean enduring very cold mornings, but it's worth more than all the silver dollars in the world.

Matt Heller (Mongolia 1995-97) is an English teacher in Bor-Undur, Mongolia, where he teaches secondary school students and facilitated a green house reconstruction project. Heller has a B.A. in English from Whitman College in Walla Walla, Washington.

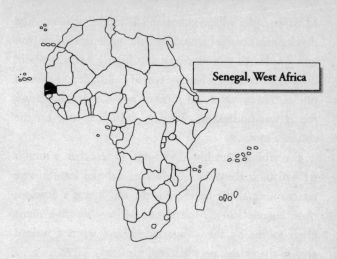

Senegal, West Africa

THE KING OF LATRINES
by Peter Halpert

I was King—King of Latrines, that is. This is the story of my quick ascent to the top and eventual downfall and personal humiliation.

I guess you could say it all started at our Peace Corps training where we were taught how to build a basic pit latrine. The simplicity of the process appealed to me. First you dig a meter-wide hole, two to three meters deep. Then you cement the walls of the hole and place a thick, round concrete slab on top. In the middle of the concrete slab is the target area, a hole six inches across.

After eight weeks of training I was assigned to a small rural village, Taiba M'Bayene, and after my arrival in Taiba

M'Bayene, the village elders and I decided that my first development project would be building latrines. The plan was simple. All those interested in having a latrine would meet at the mosque where we would build a demonstration model. There was a full turnout and the demonstration model was finished in two days, including time for the concrete to dry.

Everything went like clockwork. In less than a month we had built thirty latrines. Millet stalk enclosures were erected around the latrines for privacy. It was a development success story. Mohammed M'Baye was the name given to me by the village elders, and when I walked around the village, people hailed me.

"Mohammed M'Baye! Come into my compound. I want to show you my latrine," called Samba Gaye.

Samba Gaye was sixty years old but looked more like eighty. Even though it was at least ninety-five degrees in the shade, he had on his familiar woolen ski cap and a woolen scarf. A permanently dislocated neck made it difficult for him to talk, but that never stopped him. His words came out in sharp bursts, and his voice was high and shrill.

"Mohammed M'Baye, you have done the incredible for us. You may be here for only two years but these latrines will be here until the end of time." I thanked him and walked away, smiling at the thought of my legacy to the village. Maybe they wouldn't last until the end of time, but certainly the latrines would be there for many years.

And so it continued. Wherever I went in the village, I

would be thanked in the effusive manner of the Senegalese. My neighbor, Bi Saye, told me, "I had a guest here yesterday and instead of sending him off to the bush with his kettle, I told him to step right this way and showed him my latrine. I felt like a king. Thank you, Mohammed M'Baye, for making me feel this way."

Then there was Ibra San. He told me that he loved his latrine so much that he had put a lock on it and would not allow the women and children to use it.

The dry *harmatan* winds came just before the rainy season. The sky and air became thick with dust as sand blew in from the Sahara. The dust and dryness were soon replaced by the rains and humidity. With the rains came the flies.

The fly population in the village seemed to be increasing at a maddening rate, and I quickly realized why. The villagers were not covering the small latrine holes. When people defecated in the bush, the flies concentrated there, away from the huts. The latrines were attracting the flies, and village hygiene was suffering.

This was not a good sign for the King of Latrines.

I spoke with the elders, and we decided to hold a village meeting. Covers would have to be placed on holes, and the holes would be maintained and cleaned in order to reduce the fly population. A later inspection tour revealed that most people were following the rules. I sighed with relief as the rainy season continued.

After many years of drought, the rains turned the

parched earth green almost overnight. It rained constantly. Everywhere I looked I saw water. Puddles turned into ponds and ponds into lakes. Trickles became streams and streams became rivers. One day a river of water came rushing through the village, sweeping away everything in its path, including ten homes of mud and thatch.

It was during one of the rains that my village father came into my hut, soaking wet. He was a man of wisdom and few words. He said, "Don't use your latrine. In fact, don't even go near it, it's dangerous and has been destroyed by the rain." Then he turned and abruptly left.

I was puzzled. How could the rain destroy my latrine? That afternoon, when the rain had finally subsided and I was walking in back of my hut, the latrine caught my eye. In the back of my mind I heard the warning, but curiosity got the better of me. I walked toward the latrine. Part of the millet- stalk fence had been knocked down but the slab of concrete was still there. I walked closer for a better look. On one side the earth was eroded and there was a huge, gaping hole. When the river came through the village, a stream of water had gone directly into the latrine and filled it with water, breaking one side in the process. As I stood there, the earth suddenly started to give way underneath me. In a matter of seconds, I was up to my neck in water, mud, and excrement.

I tried to get out, but struggling only made it worse. There was no solid ground to grab onto. Everywhere I reached, the earth gave way. Panic set in as I flailed around.

My arms and legs were tiring and my life was flashing before me. I saw the grief of my parents, who had cautioned me against joining the Peace Corps in the first place. I saw my hometown newspaper with the headline, "Local boy drowns in African latrine." And, worst of all, I saw a vision of other Volunteers drinking beer in a bar and my death in a latrine becoming just another story in Peace Corps lore.

With my last bit of energy I made a frantic lunge for a sapling and, holding on for dear life, slowly pulled myself out, praying that the small tree would stay rooted. Luckily, it did.

I got out the big watering can I used for bathing and took three showers. I threw my clothes into that big sink hole that had once been my latrine and never breathed a word of what had happened. The King of Latrines left Senegal with his reputation intact.

Peter Halpert (Senegal 1977-79) was a community development worker in Taiba M'Bayene, a small rural village in central Senegal, where he worked on a latrine, vegetable garden, health hut and school projects. Halpert has an M.S. in Development Management from American University and is now living and working in Morocco on a Family Planning and Maternal Child Health Project with the U.S. Agency for International Development.

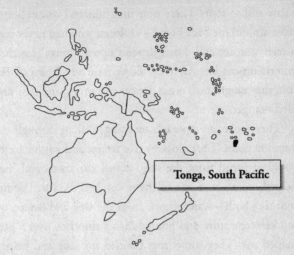

Tonga, South Pacific

UNDER THE TONGAN SUN
by Tina Martin

On Tonga, I lived in a tiny hut made of bamboo and coconut leaves and lined with dozens of mats, pieces of *tapa* cloth, and wall-to-wall children. When I sat on the floor with my back against the rear door, my feet almost touched the front door. There was no electricity or running water, so I used a kerosene lamp and drew water from the well. There were breadfruit trees and avocado trees around my hut, and if I wanted a coconut, the children climbed a tree for me.

The kids I taught were always with me, and I loved them even more than I once loved my privacy. I always wanted to have children, but I never thought I'd have so many and so soon. These were the children I would like to have around me back home—children who had never seen a television set and didn't depend upon "things" for their entertainment because they didn't *have* any "things." For fun, they taught each other dances and songs, and they juggled oranges.

They woke me up each morning, calling through my bamboo poles. They took my five *sentini* and got me freshly-baked bread from the shop across the lawn, and they helped me eat it. Some of them watched the ritual of my morning bath—water drawn from the well and heated on my kerosene stove and poured into a tin, then over a pre-soaped me. They sometimes braided my hair and helped me get dressed for school. Then they walked me there, where I used the oral English method we learned in training—acting out the language so there's no need for translation.

"I'm running! I'm running!" I said as I ran in front of the class. "I'm running! I'm running!" I took a child by the hand.

"Run!" I said, and eventually he did. The goal was to have a running paradigm, which usually ended, "I running, you running, he/she/it running." We did this for all verbs. English was the link between Tonga and all other land masses of the world. And English was the exercise that kept me scrawny, the worst physical defect a body could have in the Tongan culture, where fat is beautiful. I tried to compensate for my lack of bulk by being very *anga lelei* (good-natured), which was their most cherished personality trait.

After school, the children would come home with me and stay, singing Tongan songs and the ones I'd taught them.

Then I tried to help them prepare for the sixth-grade exam that would determine their scholastic future. And they helped me prepare whichever vegetable was to be my dinner.

The children never left until I was safely tucked into bed under my canopy of mosquito net on top of *tapa* cloth. Then I blew out my lamp, lay down, and listened to the songs from a *kava* ceremony nearby. Sometimes there was light from what a Tongan teacher told me was now the American moon, since we had put a man there.

On moonless nights, I fell asleep in complete darkness. But I fell asleep knowing that I would always wake up under the Tongan sun.

Tina Martin (Tonga 1969-71) began her career in English as a Second Language teacher trainer Volunteer in Tonga. After her service in the Peace Corps, she went on to teach in Spain and in Algeria. She is now an English as a Second Language instructor at City College of San Francisco.

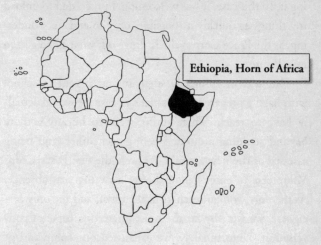

Ethiopia, Horn of Africa

THE PINK ERASER
by Kate Collins

After driving for ten hours and passing several small villages, I was convinced that the next stop had to be Arjo. And, after two more villages, it was. On the way into town, Arjo appears to be a fairly large village with clusters of tin-roofed houses lining the gravel road. It is only upon passing through the town in a matter of five minutes that one realizes just how small it is.

As soon as the car stopped, what seemed like the whole village, or at least everyone under twelve, came out to watch the *ferenji* unload all her worldly goods. *Ferenji* is a term used to describe anyone who is not Ethiopian. It can be welcoming, hostile, or comical depending on who's saying it. In this case, it was welcoming. I proceeded to unload my things as quickly as possible, only to end up wondering, as the Peace Corps vehicle drove off, what I had gotten myself into.

The next morning my sitemate and I went to school with hastily prepared lesson plans in case we would actually have to teach. There didn't seem to be any activity beyond standing around, greeting each other, and being assessed as the new arrivals. We were the first Peace Corps Volunteers to enter Ethiopia after a twenty-year absence. As the only women teachers in the town, and the only foreigners, we were by far the most interesting topic of conversation. Unfortunately, we exhausted our command of Oromifa, the local language, after a few exchanges. After dazzling everyone with our rehearsed lines, the gap between basic conversation and fluency became quickly apparent.

When we finally ventured into the town in search of food and entertainment, we realized that, although the town itself was very small, the youth population appeared to be growing at an alarming rate, judging by the crowd of small children that followed us. Having explored all possibilities for recreation, we returned to the school determined to start teaching.

While the other teachers competed in the Wimbledon of table tennis, we went to class armed with elaborate lesson plans and visions of an interactive classroom. The dark mud-floored room was crammed with over forty students, most sitting three to a desk, many older than me even though it was ninth grade, and all staring at the blonde-haired and blue-eyed *ferenji* who had come to teach them English. I was met with blank looks in the classroom and uproarious laughter as soon as I left.

Completely consumed with the thought of what I was going to teach, I forgot that I would also need chalk and an eraser. The first day I got by with a small stub of chalk and a piece of paper as an eraser. The next day I arrived with several pieces of chalk and a bandanna as an eraser.

Finally, I thought, things were beginning to fall into place. The students' laughter seemed to be confined to my mispronunciation of their names and a few students were starting to raise their hands and cautiously participate. After an exhausting first week, I arrived in class on Friday and realized I had forgotten my trusty bandanna. I vowed to use the board sparingly so I wouldn't actually have to erase anything. Obviously flustered, I continued the lesson as best I could and counted the minutes until the bell rang. Practically running from the classroom, I tried to put the whole week behind me and concentrate on relaxing over the weekend.

As I left the class, one of my female students came running after me, calling, "Teacher, teacher." She had yet to speak in class, and I didn't recall her name. "Teacher, duster, for you," she said as she handed me a small, pink, cloth eraser she had sewn for me. The gesture took me completely by surprise and, given the ups and downs of the previous week, I practically wept with gratitude. Despite the amused looks of my fellow teachers, I happily carried that eraser with me everywhere I went. Now I could get to work!

Kate Collins (Ethiopia 1995-97) was an education Volunteer in Ethiopia. Kate also worked to construct a latrine for the female students at her secondary school. She has a B.A. in English from Georgetown University.

Dominican Republic,
The Caribbean

NOT JUST ANY OTHER DAY
by Dianne Garyantes

I walked into the well-lit, freshly-painted office building—late, as expected. This was the custom in the
Dominican Republic; meetings always started late. As
I entered, I wiped the mud from my shoes; it had been
raining all day in the little village where I worked. A small
knot of women in faded dresses and flip-flops was huddled
in the center of a large meeting room. Maybe I had pushed
the lateness thing too far, I thought, because they were
waiting for me.

I had been asked by the local women's club to speak on
a panel for International Women's Day 1991. When I was
first approached to speak, I hesitated. This would not be a

discussion about AIDS awareness or planning a community project. I would have to say something about life, about women, about who we are and what we could become. During my past year in the village, I had been humbled by the harsh conditions around me and the grace with which people managed to live. Families worked three harvests a year in the nearby rice fields, nurtured supportive relationships with their families and neighbors, and most kept three or four sources of income flowing into the household. Who was I to speak to them about life or who they were? I decided my talk would have to be a discussion in which the women themselves would rely on their innate wisdom and worth.

It was a surprise to me that the women's club was acknowledging International Women's Day. The women in the club usually came together to be social, to trade sewing tips, to escape from the everyday events of the household. They were not politically active and did not identify themselves as a subordinate or marginalized group because they were women. My guess was that I had been asked to speak that day because I was a somewhat exotic *americana,* not because I was a woman.

My first glance into the meeting room told me my instincts were correct. All of the other panelists for the day were men. Although I knew that in the Dominican Republic men were viewed as the ones who spoke with and for authority, it was still a shock. This was International Women's Day! The day was set aside to celebrate women and our accomplishments. I was filled with a new sense of purpose as I walked to the front of the room.

When it was the *americana's* turn to speak, I asked the women in the audience to list all the essentials of life, things we all need as human beings to survive. The responses came at a rapid-fire pace: good health, shelter, food, water, children and family, clothing, medicine, education. The list went on until the poster board I was writing on was full.

Next, we circled in red the items on the list for which women in the Dominican Republic were responsible. The answers this time came more slowly. The first person to respond said that women in the Dominican Republic were responsible for caring for children and families. Another hand went up to point out that women collect water every day for drinking, cleaning, bathing, and cooking. We realized that women also are responsible for keeping the family healthy and getting medicine when someone is sick. Women also make sure that homework is done and that children are in school every day. Meals, clothing, and cleaning and maintenance of the home are also under the responsibility of women. We continued to circle items on the list until every single suggestion on the poster board was surrounded by red. The air in the room became thick with stunned silence.

I felt exhilarated and a little dazed by the enormity of our conclusion. All the items on the list were the responsibility of the women sitting in the room. Women were making daily decisions and carrying out responsibilities that were nothing less than essential to life. They were essential to life! Our list, cheerful with bright red circles, affirmed this.

As in societies and cultures everywhere, men and women in the Dominican Republic share in the responsibilities for their families, communities, and country. The difference is that women are seldom acknowledged, celebrated, or rewarded for their contributions. The women in the audience felt this lack of appreciation every day as they ate last, after their husbands and children, and rarely, if ever, shared a meal at the same table as their spouses. Instead, they sat in the kitchen at the back of the house, taking quick mouthfuls of food in between serving and cleaning up after the others. Many of the women in the audience also were raising children conceived by their husbands outside their marriage. And many had been put down or ignored all their lives. Who, after all, was the boss? Who, after all, was important?

One of the women in the audience that day was Gloria, who worked two jobs as a nurse and traveled forty kilometers in the back of a pick-up truck for one of her jobs. She also swept and mopped her house each day, raised a young son, and helped cultivate bananas, plantains, and cocoa for additional income. When the community needed help raising money to build a school, Gloria organized collections in the local church and raised more than $300 for the project.

Idaylia, who was also there that day, had a disabled left foot, yet still started each day by collecting water for her family. This meant at least three trips to and from the village's water hole, which was a quarter-mile from her house. She carried the water in a five-gallon can on top of her head and, even with her limp, she barely spilled a drop.

The silence in the room was beginning to soften. Someone giggled. Someone else spoke. Soon everyone in the audience was talking excitedly, telling jokes, and laughing, including the men on the panel. It was thrilling to watch the light shine in the women's eyes and to see it reflected and multiplied among them. It was as though they all had been a team running a relay and had just found out they had won first place. We loudly applauded ourselves and sailed out of the meeting room feeling giddy, buoyant, joyous.

The rush of pride and sense of awareness I shared with the women that afternoon comes back to me at different times during my life today. I think of it when I need a reminder of how human beings everywhere contribute each day to the well-being of our world. This happens whether we are recognized for it or not. This lesson is one of the many gifts given to me while I was a Peace Corps Volunteer in the Dominican Republic.

Dianne Garyantes (Dominican Republic 1989-91) lived in *El Pozo de Nagua* where she worked on community development projects. She has a graduate degree in Public Administration and International Development from Rutgers University, and a B.A. degree in Journalism/Political Science from Pennsylvania State University. She currently works for the Discovery Channel.

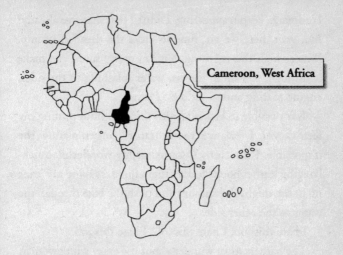

Cameroon, West Africa

DEVELOPMENT IS DOWN THIS ROAD
by Abigail Calkins

Few people recognize me without my familiar Suzuki. Now I have this red Yamaha DT they gave me to replace it. I'm still white, though. Or so they keep insisting as I pass by the shouting voices trying to get me to stop to do a favor, chat, or taste the new palm wine. I know I have a bike, but how do you say, "I'm not a taxi," in the local language? I'm late. I'm in a hurry. I've got to help a women's group plant rows of plantains and pineapple in their community farm.

This road could jostle my insides right out of me. My thighs are sore from being abused as shock absorbers. Someone must have made the road longer today; all my landmarks keep reappearing. Didn't I pass that tree already? No, wait, here we go, time to cross the dreaded swamp. Water's high this morning, but I'm pretty sure I can make it through, feet up in the air, water splashing to the sides, engine roaring and . . . it dies. Damn!

Is it possible to kick-start this thing without putting my feet down? I balance momentarily, contemplating the impossible. Reluctantly, I submerge my wonderful, quickly-aging leather boots, feeling them flood, soaking my jeans up to my thighs. I dismount and push the bike through the water to the other side.

I hate this job. I hate this job. I hate this job.

The bathers must wonder about the crazy white woman talking to herself. One little girl is crying because my yellow helmet makes me look like a monster. So I take it off. She starts shrieking. White people are ghosts. White people have funny hair and noses. White people who ride motos with helmets have strange markings of dust on their faces. Unable to pacify the kid, I shove on to the village, which is mercifully close.

The president of the women's group is waiting for me. Sloshing over to her, I pull off my gloves and helmet to embrace her. At last, we can get down to business. Drums sound nearby. Uh oh . . . not drums! Not again! Not after this hour and a half drive! Not after crossing the dreaded swamp!

The president leads me to a group of dancing women, each of whom hugs me and invites me to join them in celebration of an old man who lies dead on a cot. We dance, and I try to conceal my discomfort in celebrating death, even that of an old man. No community farms today, folks. Development will have to wait.

When the drums finally stop, the group escorts me rather officially to the president's house. They tell me they want to try making soap. This, after all, is the kind of technical know-how a white woman on a red motorcycle should have. Frankly, I don't have the first clue about soap-making.

They unknowingly introduce me to the process: lye, blanched palm oil, and three hours of stirring. The women are singing songs, songs about soap, and my heart lifts as I help them stir. Someone brings me corn-on-the-cob and warm beer. I look around. Such strength! These women with wide, open faces and old but colorful scarves wrapped around their hair, gossiping and laughing and occasionally arguing. I love this job, this job is great, I wouldn't miss this job for the world. You women are wonderful, every one of you; you make your own soap, so what if you won't work on your community farm? Soap classifies as development, doesn't it? Thunder rumbles in the distance.

It is getting late. I say, "Would it bother you if I leave now? I need to return home," and they look bothered and tell me that I must stay until the soap is finished. I oblige helplessly, pushing thunder out of my mind. More singing, stirring, and bickering, but at last the women pour the thick green soap into the square wooden mold and I take out my camera to capture the triumph. (I will say back home, "And this was the day we made soap!")

The group presents me with a gift, a splendid, singular egg, beautiful and simple. It is an egg that I will eat with joy. That is, if it makes it home intact. That is, if I make it home intact. Speaking my local-language thank yous and goodbyes, I return grimly to my red chariot. So we meet again, beast.

The swamp provides no challenge this time since my socks and jeans are still damp. My fears rest more with the deep, black mass of clouds off to my left. How fast do I have to drive to arrive home before the storm hits? If I go 264 kilometers an hour, I could be in my house in ten minutes. Chickens and children will fly. Cars will flip over behind me, and I will never even hear the fracas. Please don't rain, please don't rain, please don't rain.

The first drops splash on my nose, followed quickly by a torrential downpour, drenching me almost immediately, a cold and cruel rain, seeping beneath my kidney belt, sparing nothing. Wasn't it supposed to be warm in Africa? Swearing through my chattering teeth, I am forced to continue since there is no house in sight. Why do I do this? Why? I laugh in my ridiculous misery.

Finally, I pull into a village where some men are grilling corn on a small fire. They invite me to warm myself by it until the rain subsides. It helps. I stare out at the storm and the road; all the carefree days I glided past this village on dry dirt and never even appreciated my good fortune. Ten kilometers remain between me and my house. Streams of muddy water flood the road, redefining it. Soon it will look like chocolate frosting. Back to the bike, the helmet, and the last drizzle of rain. Home is just around the next few bends.

Abigail Calkins (Cameroon 1987-90) was a community development Volunteer in Abong-Mbang, Cameroon, where she worked with women's groups in ten villages. She has an M.A. in Public Administration/International Development from Columbia University and a B.A. in International Relations and French from Tufts University. She lives in Ciudad Juarez, Mexico, and is working for the Cooperative Housing Foundation on housing issues along the border.

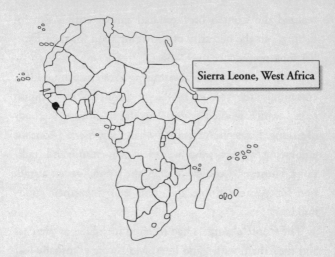

Sierra Leone, West Africa

FISHING IN SIERRA LEONE
by Phil Bob Hellmich

During my first fishing trip in West Africa, I realized a childhood dream by fighting and landing a twenty-five pound Nile perch. That happened at the end of my second year as a Peace Corps Volunteer, and it changed the rest of my time in Sierra Leone.

My main project was building a well. During the dry season, I spent the evenings fishing Sierra Leone's Rokel River with my host-country friends, the Conteh brothers—Moses, Bokarie, and Sanpha.

I caught over 125 pounds of Nile perch a month. My interest in fishing changed as my diet, and that of thirty plus Contehs, greatly improved with the fresh fish. I soon realized the Conteh brothers had similar enthusiasm for fishing, but the necessity of providing food for their families took precedence over "sport."

I was uncomfortable about using Western fishing lures, commonly referred to by Sierra Leoneans as "English baits," which worked better than the traditional methods of fishing. I was often troubled when I saw Sierra Leoneans embracing Western ways over their own culture and traditions. However, I could not deny the Contehs their attraction for Western things they had seen since their childhood.

The Conteh brothers had received such lures as presents and used them with hand lines. Most were eventually lost to large perch or the rocky bottom of the Rokel. That was a major loss, since the value of one imported lure was equal to a local teacher's monthly salary.

I lost many myself, and I replaced them from a shop 120 miles from the village. But they were expensive for me too. Several Peace Corps friends recommended that I make my own. I had never tied a fishing fly, let alone carved a stick into a fish-like lure that could dive and dance in the water. The Contehs had similar doubts, reinforced by a lack of faith in their ability to design and make a fancy "white man's" gadget.

Finally, I set for the Contehs and myself a straightforward goal: to create locally made lures that caught Nile perch and that the Conteh brothers could continue making without me. We set to work together. Within two months, Bokarie caught several Nile perch—a fish that looks like a large-mouth bass—with a lure he made himself.

Over the next twelve months:

• the Contehs became self-sufficient in making lures that attracted Nile perch;

• they began to sell their excess catch for profit;

• they successfully made their own western-style fishing reels;

• Sanpha caught 101 pounds of Nile perch in a single night;

• the Contehs served as trainers in four successful workshops;

• working together, we also developed lures that caught barracudas and worked well for salt-water fishing;

• and the Contehs started a small business, selling seventy-two lures in three months.

The plan was to use only local materials that were readily available. I did not know the local trees and their characteristics, but the Contehs knew the qualities of every tree in the bush and which tree would provide wood with the perfect buoyancy. They relied on their own carving skills to produce their everyday tools. They did not trust me with a knife for fear I would hurt myself.

The process was slow and early attempts failed miserably. Whenever we hit a problem, we would take a few days off until someone came up with an idea of how to use a local material to overcome our obstacle. This process of sharing ideas with one another was called "hanging heads," a Krio expression for group consultation.

The Conteh brothers were slow to develop pride in their work. I was more impressed with the first successful lures than they were. They said the lures were *wo-wo* (ugly). I thought they were beautiful. My Peace Corps friends shared my opinion.

One Volunteer arranged for the Conteh brothers and me to give a workshop for National Park employees. I asked the Contehs to serve as instructors. I hoped that they would gain additional skill at making lures by teaching and that they would serve as an example of Sierra Leoneans being able to make English baits. They were also better at it then I was.

After the workshop, outside interest in the Conteh brothers' work grew. The workshop stirred more discussion within the Peace Corps and the government ministry. The Contehs were still dissatisfied with their own lures and continued to ask me if I would leave them mine when I returned to the United States.

It was during the next workshop, four months later, that the Contehs finally gained a sense of pride.

The workshop came after the rainy season, a period when the Contehs were really too busy with farming to think about lures, and just before the next fishing season.

It was attended by Volunteers and Sierra Leonean development workers from around the country, twenty-one people in all. After the workshop, Moses said, "I did not believe you, Phil Bob, when you said people liked our lures, but when I saw all those important people listening to my every word, my head became bigger than my body."

The Contehs emerged from the workshop with both a sense of pride and a demand for their lures. They returned to their village just as the dry season fishing began. The "hanging heads" sessions became more frequent as the Contehs began to market lures and to fish. This was when Sanpha returned from the river one night with four Nile perch weighing 101 pounds.

After ten months of making lures, Sanpha was suddenly telling me that he had caught bigger fish than I had, and with lures that he had made himself. He also pointed out that I had never made a single lure from start to finish. We all laughed as I set to work carving my first lure.

Some while later, during my last fishing trip to the Rokel river, I came across a farmer fishing with a Conteh lure. I quietly sat back and watched as he pulled a Nile perch from the water and headed back to his village. An impossible feat had now become routine, almost casual. It was time to go home.

Phil Bob Hellmich (Sierra Leone 1985-89) was a health and rural development Volunteer in Kagbere and Masongbo, Sierre Leone, where he helped to create an appropriate technology water well project and to develop locally-made fishing lures. Hellmich has a B.A. in History from DePauw University.

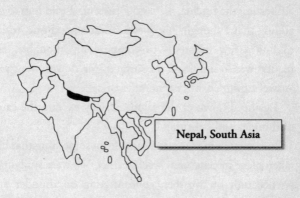

Nepal, South Asia

THUNDER AND ENLIGHTENMENT
by Duane Karlen

Every student in the class looked up at me, waiting for my answer. The room was quiet, unusually quiet for this group of boisterous twelve year-olds who rarely sat still on their creaky wooden benches and whose attention often flitted about like the sparrows that came to the open windows.

But today was exam day, and exams are serious business in Nepal. A student's grade can mean the difference between continuing in school or returning to labor in the terraced rice fields that surround the Himalayan mountain village.

Ram Gopal, who had asked the question, was still

standing, waiting for permission to resume his seat after addressing the teacher, as was the custom. I told him to sit, adding that I thought his question was a good one, trying to buy a few moments to compose my thoughts. His request was so simple on the surface: "Sir, do you want *your* answer or *our* answer on number three?"

I glanced down at the exam: "Briefly explain the cause of thunder and lightning."

I realized Ram's question came from something that had taken place in class a few weeks earlier. We were studying a science unit on weather, concentrating on thunder and lightning. The text gave a rather complicated explanation that involved atmospheric temperature gradients, rising air masses, ionic exchanges, positive and negative electronic discharges, and the speed of light versus the speed of sound. Pretty heady stuff for these young boys and girls who live far from roads and electricity!

I had tried to make the lesson more interesting and understandable by explaining it in simpler words, using demonstrations of static electricity with combs and small bits of paper, and taking the class outside to observe thunderhead clouds forming in the afternoon sky.

This was my second year teaching science in Gahonsahor, an agricultural village two days' walk east of the Pokhara airport. My command of the local alphabet had grown to where I could write on the blackboard to illustrate my diagrams, and my ear for the hill dialect allowed me to follow their discussions about what we were studying. So I was delighted one day when a student bravely asked me, "Sir, would you like to hear *our* explanation of thunder and lightning?" There was an expectant pause, with all attention on the teacher.

"Yes, tell me!" I replied, making no attempt to act like the traditional teacher who strives to be the sole source of all knowledge and academic wisdom.

What followed was one of the most exciting conversations I have ever heard in a classroom. Students eagerly took turns telling me about *Indra*, the weather god who lives in the sky. Interrupting and correcting each other in their enthusiasm, they explained how *Indra* occasionally becomes angry and throws "thunderbolts" down to earth. These flash brilliantly through the sky and strike the ground with a thunderous crash, shattering anything in the way.

These bolts are triangular pieces of rock, rather like very large arrowheads. Usually they are smashed to dust by the impact, the students told me, but once in a while one is found where lightning has struck, black, very hard, smooth like glass on the outside. They are hard to crack, but if you can break off a piece and grind it up, it's a powerful medicine that can cure many problems of the body and spirit.

I asked if anyone had ever seen such a thunderbolt. Most had only heard of them, but a couple of students knew someone who knew someone who had found one, and one student even had an uncle who might actually *have* one!

I was astonished the next day when one of the students returned to class with a small piece of rock, broken from the original triangle. He excitedly showed it to the entire group, then presented it to me as a gift from his family, to take home and use when necessary. Twenty-five years later, I still keep this treasure in a special brass bowl by my bedside, strong medicine for when I need it.

The science unit on weather had taken several weeks to cover, much longer than the four or five days I had originally scheduled. I was not sure exactly what my students had learned. I would find out from this exam. However, I certainly came away with a feeling of satisfaction that something important had happened.

But now the class was waiting for my answer to Ram's question, and I felt as if I was the one being tested. My reply would tell them how much I understood their culture and accepted what was important to them. Who is "right" here? If the students accept "my" scientific concepts, are they turning their backs on their own heritage? Is my work here then undermining the very cultural uniqueness I have learned to respect? On the other hand, if they assume "their" answer is correct, are they really learning science? I needed a flash of inspiration.

I focused again on my students. There was no ambivalence in their faces. These children were easily able to grasp both sets of beliefs without a problem. One they explored in their classroom, the other was a part of their religion and folklore. Both made sense, both were acceptable. At this moment all they wanted to know was: which would be the correct answer on the test?

I spoke without further hesitation. "Since this is a science exam, give the scientific explanation. In Hindu culture class, you could give the explanation that involves Indra. But here let's use the one that comes from our textbook."

Relieved at having the issue clarified, the students resumed writing, concentrating on their sentences, occasionally gazing out the window to gather their thoughts. I sat quietly, watching them with fond amazement. Far off in the mountains, signaling the development of an afternoon storm, there was a faint rumble of thunder.

Duane Karlen (Nepal 1970-72) taught science and mathematics in a secondary school in rural Nepal. That experience changed his focus of interest from science to human behavior. He went on to a career in counseling, management training, and organizational consulting. Returning to the Peace Corps in 1991, he currently works at headquarters in Washington, D.C.

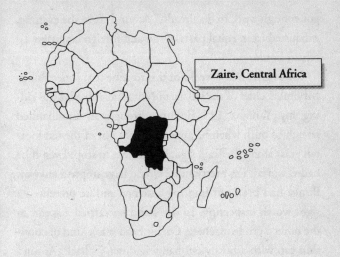

Zaire, Central Africa

THE JOY OF DIGGING
by Mike Tidwell

Equipped with a motorcycle from the United States Agency for International Development and administrative support from the Zairian Department of Agriculture and Rural Development, I set out to show the people of Kalambayi something about fish culture. I was an extension agent for the government's *Project Pisciculture Familiale.*

Six days a week, I left my house around seven o'clock in the morning and rode as much as forty miles over unspeakably eroded dirt roads and down narrow paths. I visited villages and expounded on the virtues of fish culture to anyone who would listen. "No, thanks," they often said, "we've got enough work to do already." Around six in the evening, exhausted from equal parts of sun and foreign language, I'd return home.

It was after a few weeks of this routine that I met Ilunga Mbumba, chief of the village of Ntita Kalambayi. I was riding my Yamaha 125 Enduro through an uninhabited stretch of bush when he appeared from out of the ten foot-tall grass along the trail, signaling for me to stop. Even if he hadn't waved, I'm pretty sure I would have stopped anyway. Ilunga had been out hunting antelope and he presented a sight worth inspecting. In one hand he carried a spear, in the other a crude machete. On his head was a kind of coonskin cap with a bushy tail hanging down in back. Around his neck hung a string with a leather charm to ward off evil bush spirits. Two underfed mongrel dogs circled his bare feet, panting.

When I saw Ilunga that first time, I saw a man living, it seemed to me, in another century. Inside the tall grass from which he had just stepped, the clock ran a thousand years slow, if it registered any time at all. Unable to help myself, I openly stared at him, taking him in from head to toe. He, meanwhile, stared back at me with the same wide-eyed incredulity. And no wonder. With my ghost-white skin and rumbling motorcycle, with my bulging safety goggles and orange riding gloves, with my bushy brown beard flowing out from under a banana-yellow crash helmet—with all this, I suppose I had a lot of nerve thinking of *him* as a museum piece.

For a moment we just kept gawking, Ilunga and I, mentally circling each other, each of us trying to decide whether to burst out laughing or to run for safety. In the end, we did neither. We became friends.

"My name is Ilunga," he said, extending his hand.

"My name is Michel," I said. We shook hands.

We smiled at each other some more before Ilunga got around to telling me he had heard my job was to teach people how to raise fish. It sounded like something worth trying, he said, and he wondered if I would come by his village to help him look for a pond site. I said I would and took down directions to his house.

The next day, the two of us set off into the bush, hunting for a place to raise fish.

"The first thing we need," I told Ilunga, "is water. Do you know a good spot where there's a small stream or a spring?"

"Follow me," he said.

Machetes in hand, we stomped and stumbled and hacked our way through the savanna grass for two hours before finding an acceptable site along a stream about a twenty-minute walk from Ilunga's village. Together, we measured off a pond and staked out a water canal that would run between it and a point farther up the stream. Then, with a shovel I sold him on credit against his next corn harvest, Ilunga began a two-month journey through dark caverns of physical pain and overexertion. He began digging. No bulldozers here. The task of carving out a pond from the valley-bottom floor was left to the farmer himself.

There is no easy way to dig a fish pond with a shovel. You just have to do it. You have to place the tip to the ground, push the shovel in with your foot, pull up a load of dirt, and then throw the load twenty or thirty feet to the pond's edge. Then you have to do it again—tip to the ground, push it in, pull it up, throw the dirt. After you do this about 50,000 times, you have an average-size, ten-by fifteen-meter pond.

But Ilunga, since he was a chief, wasn't going to be content with an average-size pond. He wanted one almost twice that size. He wanted a pond fifteen-by-twenty meters. I told him he was crazy as we measured it out. I repeated the point with added conviction after watching him use his bare foot to drive the thin shovel blade into the ground.

"A pond this big is too much work for one person," I said. "It'll kill you."

"See you next week," he said.

"It's too much, Ilunga."

He started digging.

"Okay," I said. *"Bonne chance."*

I left him at the pond site and began heading toward the village, hearing every ten seconds as I walked away the sound of a shovel-load of dirt hitting the ground after traveling twenty feet through the air.

For me, it was painful visiting Ilunga each week. This

was the part of the fish-culture process I had been dreading ever since arriving. I'd come by to check on the pond's progress and find Ilunga grunting and shoveling and pitching dirt the same way I had left him the week before. I calculated that to finish the pond he would have to move a total of 4,000 cubic feet of dirt. Guilt gnawed at me. This was no joke. He really was going to kill himself.

One week I couldn't stand it any longer. I found Ilunga at the pond site with his body covered with the usual mixture of dirt and sweat.

"Give me the shovel," I told him.

"Oh no, Michel," he said. "This work is too much for you."

"Give it to me," I repeated, a bit indignantly. "Take a rest."

He shrugged and handed me the shovel. I began digging. Okay, I thought, tip to the ground, push it in, pull it up, throw the dirt. I did it again. It wasn't nearly as hard as I had thought. Stroke after stroke, I kept going. About twenty minutes later, though, it got hot. I began wondering how, at 8:30 in the morning, the sun had suddenly reached noontime intensity. I paused to take off my shirt. Ilunga, thinking I was quitting, jumped up and reached for the shovel.

"No, no," I said. "I'm still digging. Sit down."

He shrugged again and said that since I was apparently serious about digging, he was going to go check on one of his fields. "Good idea," I said.

Shirtless, alone, I carried on. Tip to the ground, push it in, pull it up, throw the dirt. An hour passed. Tip to the ground, push it in, pull it up . . . throw . . . throw the . . . dammit, throw the dirt. My arms were signaling that they didn't like tossing dirt over such a great distance. But I couldn't stop. I had been digging for only an hour and a half. I was determined to go on, to help Ilunga. How could I expect villagers to do work I was incapable of doing myself?

Sweat gathered on my forehead and streamed down my face as I continued, shoveling and shoveling. Another thirty minutes passed and things started to get really ugly. My body buckled with fatigue. My back and shoulders joined my arms in screaming for an end to hostilities. I was no longer able to throw the dirt. Instead, I carried each load twenty feet and ignobly dumped it onto the dike. I was glad Ilunga wasn't around to see this. It was embarrassing. And, God, was it hot. The hottest day I could remember. Even occasional breezes rustling through the surrounding savanna grass didn't help. And then I looked at my hands. Both palms had become blistered. One was bleeding.

I took a short break and then began digging again. The pain resumed, cracking out all over my body. Fifteen minutes later, my hands finally refused to grip the shovel. It fell to the ground. My back refused to bend. I was whipped. After just two hours of digging, I was incapable of doing any more. With a stiff, unnatural walk, I went over to the dike. Ilunga had just returned, and I collapsed next to him.

"I think I'll stop now," I managed, unable to hide my pitiful state. "Take over if you want."

He did. He stood up, grabbed the shovel and began working—smoothly, confidently, a man inured to hard work. Tip to the ground, push it in, pull it up, throw the dirt. Lying on my side, exhausted, I watched Ilunga. Then I looked hard at the spot where I had been digging. I had done nothing. The hole was essentially unchanged. I had moved perhaps thirty cubic feet of dirt. That meant 3,970 cubic feet for Ilunga.

After the brief digging experience, my weekly visits to the pond became even more painful and my awe of Ilunga grew. Day after day, four or five hours each day, he kept going. He kept digging his pond. He worked like a bull and never complained. Not once. Not when he hit a patch of rocks that required a pickaxe and extra sweat. Not when, at the enormous pond's center, he had to throw each shovel-load twice to reach the dikes. Not even when he became ill.

His hand was on fire one morning when I arrived and shook it.

"You're sick," I said.

"I know," he said, and resumed digging.

"Then quit working and get some rest."

"I can't," came the reply. "I've got to finish this pond."

Several weeks later, Ilunga drove his shovel into the earth and threw its load one last time. I never thought it would happen, but there it was: Ilunga's pond, huge, fifteen-by-twenty meters, and completely finished. We hollowed out a bamboo inlet pipe and positioned it in the upper dike so canal water could enter the pond. Three days later, the pond was gloriously full of water. Using my motorcycle and two ten-liter carrying *bidons,* I transported stocking fish from another project post twenty miles to the south. When the last of the 300 *tilapia* fingerlings had entered the new pond, I turned to Ilunga and shook his hand over and over again. We ran around the banks hooting and hollering, laughing like children, watching the fish and marveling at what a wonderful thing a pond was.

To celebrate, I had brought a bottle of *tshitshampa,* the local home brew, and Ilunga and I began pouring each other shots, slapping each other on the back, and talking entirely too loud for two men sitting alone on a pond bank in the middle of the African bush. A warm glow from the drink spread from our stomachs to our limbs and, soon, strongly, our heads. Ilunga talked about his dream of digging three, six, twelve more fish ponds, and I concluded that there was no biological reason why, if fed properly, *tilapia* couldn't grow to be the size of Land Rovers. At one point, we decided to assign names to all of Ilunga's fish. Straight-faced, signaling each other to be quiet, we crouched next to the water and began naming the first few fish that swam by. After four fish, though, we lost track of which fish had which names. This struck us as absolutely hilarious, and we fell on our backs and stamped our feet and laughed so hard it hurt.

Oh, sweet joy, the pond was finished. Ilunga had done

it. He had taken my instructions and accomplished something important. And on that day when we finally stocked the pond, I knew that no man would ever command more respect from me than one who, to better feed his children, moves 4,000 cubic feet of dirt with a shovel.

Mike Tidwell (Zaire 1985-87) is the author of *The Ponds of Kalambayi*, a book about his Peace Corps experience that won the 1991 Paul Cowan Prize given by *RPCV Writers & Readers*. He is also author of *In The Shadow of the White House: Drugs, Death, and Redemption on the Streets of the Nation's Capital*, and *Amazon Stranger*.

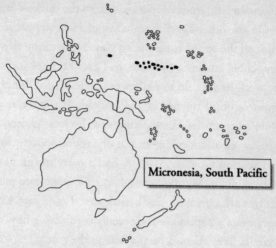

Micronesia, South Pacific

ISLAND GHOSTS
by Gardner D. Smith

Ghosts are taken very, very seriously on Fefen, an island in Chuuk, Micronesia. They can come in many different forms, from old, child-devouring men to beautiful women who lure young men into the mangrove swamps to drown. They can trick you into giving up your land or teach valuable lessons about loyalty, honesty, and sharing food.

Or they can just scare the hell out of you.

I'm not a big believer in ghosts, despite the stories of apparitions in Japanese bunkers from the second World War, the tricksters who shake the trees and make the bread-fruit and coconuts fall in your path, or the ghost of the mountain who leads people astray into the thickest jungle.

On the other hand, I am a fan of Halloween, the day when all the spirits come out to play. None of my elementary school students, however, had ever heard of it. So, in the week leading up to Halloween, I decided to build my lessons around themes of the undead. We made masks, wrote scary stories, drew pictures of the local ghosts, and even carved a jack-o-lantern out of a round watermelon.

Then, on October 31st, we had a party in the *uut*, or meeting place. My mother had sent me some face paints, candy, and a freakish devil mask that I was sure would cause quite a commotion, especially considering how missionaries have affected people here in the past.

To start out, some of the teachers told ghost stories in Chuukese. The students from grades one through eight were enthralled. This is how education here should be, I thought, especially in this oral culture. It didn't matter just then that our school didn't have walls, or electricity, or basic materials. What mattered was the passing on of knowledge, history, and values, all through stories.

Afterward, when all the kids were primed for scaring, I came flying in wearing the devil mask and a *lava lava* cape, roaring for all I was worth. The reaction was a little more than I expected. Half the first graders ran away. Some ran all the way home. Some didn't come back. I chased the rest all over the place and roared myself hoarse. After a while, the kids remembered to shout, "Trick or Treat," and I threw the candy to them. The other teachers painted their faces as ghouls and chased the children around some more. Then we ate and we sang and we danced.

That night I visited with some of the families whose kids had run away. We all laughed about it and shared more stories.

But on the way home the strangest thing happened. The huge mango tree near our house shook and the leaves fluttered violently. But there was no wind. No wind at all.

Gardner D. Smith (Micronesia 1995-97) is a teacher at UFO Elementary School in Chuuk, Micronesia. He has an M.S. in Elementary Education from the College of St. Rose and a B.A. in English from Colgate University.

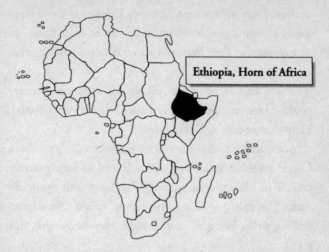

Ethiopia, Horn of Africa

THE RIGHT WAY TO GROW TOMATOES
by Karen DeWitt

I'd forgotten that I had even taken the Peace Corps recruitment test when that long-distance call came on a cold January day in 1965. Then, standing in a battered wooden telephone booth in my dormitory at Miami University of Ohio, I heard someone say, "Congratulations. You've been accepted."

Suddenly graduate school, job, the ordinary future that stretched before me and my classmates disappeared, replaced by adventure, excitement, and the unknown—literally the unknown, for I hadn't even asked what country I would be stationed in. Didn't know, didn't care.

Suddenly, I was to be part of an adventure for my generation. I was to become a Kennedy kid, one of those thousands of young people whom he had asked to dedicate one or two years of their lives to work in Africa, Latin America, or Asia.

It was a heady invitation, asking not what your country could do for you, but what you could do for your country. Here was something I could do.

According to the television commercials, the Peace Corps involved scrabbling up hills and swinging across ravines in Marine-style training, laughing with exotically dressed peoples, speaking in strange tongues, teaching, drilling wells, living in mud houses. Hey—now that was me!

The first letter from the Peace Corps told me I was going to Turkey. Great. I'd never been to Turkey. A second letter corrected the first; I was going to India. Cool. A third letter said East Africa—Ethiopia, to be specific. Wonderful. I found Ethiopia on a map, then sought out the sole Ethiopian student on campus. He was amused by my enthusiasm. Only a short while ago I hadn't known he existed. Now I was fumbling around in his language, ravenous for information about his culture and customs.

The Peace Corps did a great job of training me. Eighteen months after that telephone call, with three months of living and teaching in the "culturally different" East Los Angeles barrio, and a month of in-country training under my belt, I was a teacher of English. And thanks to months of language training, I arrived in the highland village of Ghion armed with a great deal of Amharic, Ethiopia's national language, though that never prevented me from saying the word "yellow" when I meant "only."

I had expected, in my arrogance and ignorance, that I would give more than I got. I didn't. And my life has been the richer for it. I learned things profound and mundane: that a real "free-range" chicken is a tough bird to fry; that you get a heap of liver from a freshly slaughtered cow; that growing tomatoes in a frame is far superior to staking them, as I'd always been taught; that Africa is mighty cold at 8,000 feet above sea level; that I had a gift for teaching.

As a student, I confess I was less successful. In an effort to quit smoking, I decided to learn to spin cotton. A deft Ethiopian woman named Conjeet tried for months to teach me, but never quite succeeded. Holding her spindle—which looked like an old-fashioned wooden baby rattle—in one hand, and darting it in and out of a puff of cotton, Conjeet spun threads as fine as any I'd ever pulled from a commercial spool. It looked so easy. I spun rope, I spun twine, I spun cord, I spun cable, but I never produced a thread as fine as Conjeet's. Her friends would come night after night to watch the *ferenji* (foreign woman) spin, giggling at my efforts. They were sure I'd never get a husband.

"You spin like a man," laughed Conjeet. And so, instead of the sheer white shawl worn by Ethiopian women, the village weaver made a gabi, a heavy man's garment, from my thread. I wore it the whole time I was in Ethiopia.

I had great admiration for much that I met with in

Ethiopia. But I never tried to become Ethiopian because there was always some aspect of the culture that didn't suit me. I was an incurable American.

Shortly after my arrival in Ghion, my neighbor, Ato Getachew, an important landlord in the area, invited me for a meal and did something that horrified me. He picked among the leftover bones from the stew we had eaten, and with the hauteur of a king, offered one to his son. The boy shuffled forward, eyes lowered, his left hand politely holding the wrist of his outstretched right hand.

The boy scuttled back to his corner to gnaw on the bone like a dog. This was a perfectly acceptable way to treat a child by traditional Ethiopian standards, but it shocked me.

However, I did encounter Third World justice in a very satisfactory form on an Ethiopian bus. Buses were always crowded, and in order to make a second run back to the capital before nightfall, the buses on my route often doubled up passengers from one bus to another at a village halfway to Ghion. The little Russian-built buses had a capacity of thirty passengers, but there were often twice as many people crammed aboard. Women and children were the first to suffer. Ousted from their seats, they ended up on the floor as men jammed into their places. I'd seen this many times, but on this day I shouted to the driver that this was unjust, illegal, and unsafe. He laughed. Frustrated, I told him that he could do what he liked but the farmer who sat beside me and I were going to be the sole occupants of our seat.

At that moment, a well-filled-out man of status, a *teliq saw* (important man), clambered onto the bus, the last to board. He surveyed the passengers. He shoved the poor farmer away and took his seat. I told the *teliq saw* he could not do that. He laughed at me. He said he was a lawyer from Addis Ababa. Using an informal Amharic reserved for children and servants, he told me to mind my own business.

I let my great granny's Irish temper get the best of me. I told him a good many things about himself, and then I suggested he get up. He laughed again. I stabbed the tip of my umbrella into his thigh.

He got up. He stayed up. The poor farmer, far from thankful at the return of his seat, balanced nervously at its far edge, as far away from the crazy *ferenji* as possible.

Until the bus pulled into Ghion, the lawyer lectured the passengers on the evils of Peace Corps Volunteers, the low morals of American women, the bad examples we were to his country's women and children, and how we had no jobs in the United States and had come to Ethiopia to eat meat every day. He was going to have me put into jail, he announced.

When the bus reached Ghion, the lawyer grabbed my arm and told me that I was going to the police station. I shook him off. He grabbed me again. Right there in the middle of Ghion's main thoroughfare, that lawyer and I began fighting. I slashed away at him with my umbrella, like some mad black Mary Poppins. By now, it was night, the hour of the evening stroll, and we attracted a crowd, including many students from my school. Eventually we attracted the police.

Lawyer, police, crowd, and I went off to the police station. After much discussion, the police jailed the Addis lawyer. He wasn't from the town. I was.

The Amharic word I heard most often during my time in Ethiopia was *ferenji*—foreign woman. Whether spoken affectionately or harshly, the word reminded me that I was *in* the country but not *of* it. No matter that I was fluent in the local language, ate only local food, was godparent to a villager's child, and buddy to the local moonshiner, I was still the foreigner. But that wasn't true that night. I was the *yesalem guad* (Peace Corps) from Ghion. I belonged there, and the out-of-town lawyer did not.

The next day, my students wanted to know how I dared to do what I had done. I was a woman; he was a man. True, I was a teacher, a position with status, but he was a lawyer. I lived in a little provincial village, while he was from the capital. I was young then, so I used the incident to teach a lesson in democracy, the principles of social equality, and respect for the individual within the community, regardless of status and power.

I don't know whether I did them a favor or not. I don't know if the experience wasn't more valuable to me than to the local people. I don't even know, now, if I acted with the best motives—standing up against injustice—or whether I wasn't just an ignorant and arrogant American, annoyed at being inconvenienced.

What I do know is that the whole experience made me adventurous and eager for more. For more culture, more countries, more languages, more roads and vistas, more smells, sounds, and experiences beyond those of my own country. My years in the Peace Corps gave me a perspective from which to understand different attitudes toward time, to appreciate the slowness of a Malaysian fashion show, and to understand that there is more than one right way to do things, including growing tomatoes.

Karen DeWitt (Ethiopia 1966-68) has been a reporter for *The Washington Post, USA TODAY,* and is currently with the Washington Bureau of *The New York Times.* She is a regular guest on "To The Contrary" on PBS.

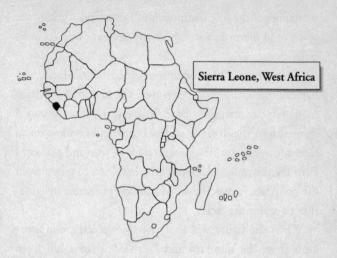

Sierra Leone, West Africa

LEAVING A LEGACY
by Gary Schulze

T he famous Temne warrior, Bai Bureh, was known to everyone in Sierra Leone because he'd led a protest against the British in 1898 after the colonial government tried to enforce a hut tax. The only existing picture of the warrior was a pencil drawing made by an English policeman after Bai Bureh had been taken into custody. It showed him in profile sitting on a box. The drawing had been printed in a turn-of-the-century book written by T. J. Aldridge.

As the acting curator of the Sierra Leone Museum at the Cotton Tree, I thought it might be nice to have a life-size figure of Bai Bureh in the museum. It was 1962, and I was a member of the first contingent of Peace Corps Volunteers to serve in Sierra Leone, which had recently won its independence.

There was a Creole sculptor named J. D. Marsh who lived on the outskirts of Freetown, the capital. Mr. Marsh made life-size statues of dead people to place on graves. I showed him the drawing of Bai Bureh and commissioned him to construct a life-size figure out of wire and plaster of Paris for the museum. Because he had little to go on from the policeman's sketch, Mr. Marsh had to use his imagination to sculpt the face.

When the figure was ready two weeks later, two assistants from the museum and I carried it up a hill from Marsh's workshop to a taxi. Since the statue had been painted dark brown and was wrapped in rough cloth, people thought we were carrying away a human corpse. Old women started wailing and clapping their hands as we passed. In the museum, I dressed the figure in an old, authentic Temne warrior's cap and hunting jacket and wired an antique sword from the 1890s to his right hand.

In the next few months, thousands of people came to the museum to see Bai Bureh. In subsequent years, photographs of the figure began to appear in Sierra Leone history books. The statue was displayed at agricultural shows and other events around the country.

In October 1993, thirty years after I'd completed my Peace Corps tour, I returned to Sierra Leone. To my surprise, Bai Bureh was still standing in the museum, looking proud albeit a little worn; some of the paint had peeled off and his right arm was broken, with wire and plaster hanging from where the sword was attached.

Soon after I returned to the United States, the Bank of Sierra Leone issued new currency. A friend of mine in Europe, Bill Hart, sent me the new Le. 1,000 note, which features an etching of Mr. Marsh's rendition of Bai Bureh, still wearing the hat with tassels I placed on his head more than thirty years ago.

Last year I went back to Sierra Leone as a member of the United Nations International Observer team for the country's presidential and legislative elections. Bai Bureh was not only still standing in the museum, but life-size replicas of the statue could be found in the lobbies of several hotels in Freetown. Miniature copies of the statue, complete with cap and sword, were sold all over the city as souvenirs. Moreover, the carvers had invented a female companion, *Mrs.* Bai Bureh.

As Bill Hart told me in his letter, I may be the only Peace Corps Volunteer who ever influenced the currency of the country in which he served. And as for the late Mr. Marsh, he put a face on one of Sierra Leone's most famous heroes.

Gary Schulze (Sierra Leone 1961-63) was a secondary school teacher at Albert Academy in Freetown where he taught history and civics. He also served as acting curator of the Sierra Leone National Museum. Schulze has an M.A. in Foreign Political Institutions from Columbia University and a B.A. in Government and Psychology from New York University.

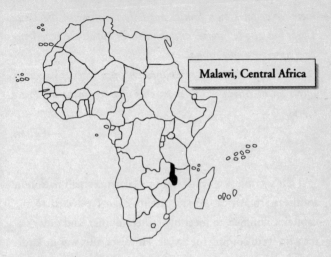

Malawi, Central Africa

FAMILY AFFAIR
By Tana Beverwyk

S argent Shriver, first Director of the Peace Corps, liked to say that the real beneficiaries of the Peace Corps would be the children of Volunteers. He meant that former Volunteers would raise their children differently because of the experience. Little did Shriver realize, back in the early 1960s, that for many families Peace Corps service itself would become a legacy. Someday the kids may inherit the family business, the attic antiques, even the homestead. But first, maybe, they'd join the Peace Corps.

The Peace Corps has found over the years that it is former Volunteers who make the best recruiters, and they are especially successful at recruiting other family members. Having a *member of one's own family not only recommend the Peace Corps but also tell stories and show slides makes the experience very up-close and personal.*

This essay demonstrates what can happen when a Volunteer meets up in Africa with her parents who served in the Peace Corps.

—Editors

I am serving as a Volunteer in Malawi, a small nation in southeastern Africa. Several months ago I traveled to the capital, Lilongwe, to meet my father, mother, and older sister who were coming for a visit. However, this was no ordinary visit, since my family had left Africa twenty-six years ago and was returning for the first time.

My mother and father had both served as Peace Corps Volunteers in Kenya in 1969-70. They were newlyweds. My sister was born during their time of service. (Peace Corps policy was a little more relaxed about pregnant Volunteers back then.) Those two years in the Peace Corps changed my parents' lives and, subsequently, changed my own. Everything, from their decision to make a home in northern New Mexico because it looked and felt like East Africa, to raising their children as global citizens, resulted from their time working as secondary-school teachers in Kenya.

The first part of our time together here in Malawi was spent exploring. It was wonderful to share with them the beauty of Malawi and its people. They were sharply reminded of the unique life of a Volunteer: the lonely silence of a rural village, the frustrating cross-cultural struggles at work, the stress-relieving parties that erupt when Volunteers get together. All of this took them back to a time when they, too, ran to jump on a crowded country bus and struggled with this life they had chosen.

The apex of their homecoming to Africa, however, was our journey to a tiny village in Nyanza Province of southwestern Kenya. Taran'ganya was the place where they had lived and served as Volunteers so many years ago. Their first contact with the past was with one former student they had taught as Volunteers, now a highly respected professor in Nairobi, who had kept in contact throughout the years. He opened his home to us with great pride, having, as he sincerely said, "finally the chance to give back a little of what his Peace Corps teachers had given to him."

He took over all the arrangements for our trip to Kuria District to visit Taran'ganya Secondary School and many of his former classmates. The 350-mile trip was filled with memories for my parents: the dirt roads where they had desperately hitched rides when they were my age; the market where they bought bananas, powdered milk, and, occasionally, fresh meat; the people speaking a mix of Kiswahili, Kikuria, and English. For my sister and me, it provided a sharp realization of the impact that those two years had had on our parents, as well as proof that the Peace Corps adventure stories we had grown up hearing were, indeed, true.

Their region had changed and prospered in twenty-six years, just like the rest of Kenya. Their small school was now twice the size it had been in 1969. Its whitewashed buildings housed hundreds of anxious-faced students still learning out of old, dingy textbooks. As we walked into the schoolyard, students and teachers excitedly rushed out to see why the four *wazungu* (white people), accompanied by the well-known professor, were visiting their school. My parents were beaming as they spoke with these students who were so much like those they had taught, in that same small place, twenty-six years before.

We spent the next three days in Kuria visiting former students who had remained in their tribal district. I wish I could describe the rush of emotions experienced by mom and dad. To see their former students, schoolboys who could barely afford a pair of shoes, as professional adults with grown families was quite overwhelming for them.

The first student we visited was now the chief of a major Kuria village. He cried out with amazement at seeing his teachers again, and, over warm Fanta and biscuits, told stories about how my parents had changed his life. He spoke of spending hours at their house reading Mark Twain. He thanked their influence for his decision not to have his six daughters sent for female circumcision, still widely practiced among the Kuria people. My parents had no idea that their influence had been so profound on the quiet boy who would read in their house until the paraffin lamp ran out of fuel. It was so profound, in fact, that he had grown into an influential man who would begin, by daring example, to end a harmful practice among his people.

We then visited another former student who had become a successful doctor. He had chosen to stay in his town to practice medicine and to build a hospital, the region's first. Never have I seen the eyes of a grown man light up as much as his when he realized who the gray-haired people standing before him were. He was chattering immediately about the powerful influence mom and dad had had on him. He talked about the boxing and track clubs dad had started, and attributed the fact that he now writes in only capital letters to his trying to emulate the writing of his old Peace Corps teacher. He could hardly believe that the twenty-five-year-old woman in front of him was the same tiny baby to whom he and his friends had brought gifts when she was born. She was the first white baby they had ever seen.

And, finally, on our way back to Nairobi, we stopped at a small public health clinic in the town of Migori to visit the old medical assistant who had worked in the village near the school. He had given my father an injection to treat a bout of malaria twenty-six years ago. After the usual tears and delighted chatter, he took my mom's hand and led her to the back of the clinic. There he produced a medical text that she had given him as a gift before her tour in the Peace Corps ended. For all these years, it was the only training manual for the laboratory staff of the clinic. The book was now tattered and torn but was still serving a purpose my mother could not have imagined when she passed it on.

The point of these reflections is that my parents had absolutely no idea how much influence they were having during their two years of Peace Corps service. They did not consider themselves exceptional Volunteers; they simply went to class, taught a variety of subjects in the best way they knew how, and loved the people they lived among. But returning to their village so many years later, they were struck by the undeniable realization that they had indeed changed people's lives.

Seeing how these former students reacted to my parents was incredible, persuasive evidence that Peace Corps Volunteers have a profound influence wherever they go, whatever they do. In fact, I felt that a Volunteer could almost spend the entire two years of service locked inside a house and still change something significant in the lives of people all around.

Tana Elizabeth Beverwyk (Malawi 1995-98) is an AIDS Education Volunteer in Mpherembe, Malawi. She has a B.A. in Communications Arts and Sciences from Michigan State University.

Paraguay, South America

MAY THE CIRCLE BE UNBROKEN
by John Garamendi

At the customs area in the Asunción Airport, I wait anxiously for my luggage, loaded down with Christmas presents. At last, I pass through customs and greet my son, John, and his wife, Colleen, who are in Paraguay as Peace Corps Volunteers. We hug and kiss, even shed a few tears. I am proud of them and the commitment they've made. I'm glad to see them and eager to find out first-hand about their lives.

In a cab, we ride past fancy suburbs with high walls, past big houses, and European and American stores and auto dealerships to the old town, with its narrow streets, dirty gutters, and crumbling sidewalks. We enter the Shara Hotel, a Peace Corps crash house. Six bucks per person, a good price even if it doesn't include a working air-conditioner.

I remember my own days as a Peace Corps Volunteer thirty years ago in Ethiopia: cheap hotels in the old quarter of Addis Ababa; slow-moving ceiling fans stirring humid air; noisy patrons at the local bars across the street; narrow beds with thin mattresses that sagged like the backs of old donkeys carrying water in the village. Memories of Patti, my wife, a bright-eyed, eager woman lying next to me, unable to sleep as she analyzes the problems of our village and conjures up answers that dissolve in the *swish, swish, swish* of the fan blades overhead. But hope is miraculously restored the next morning. We awake eager to return to the village, to seize the day and get on with the towering task.

The next morning, John and Colleen show me Asunción, filling me in on its history, and I remember how Patti and I escorted my own parents through Addis Ababa when we were Volunteers. We, too, gave my parents a similar lecture.

To reach John and Colleen's village, I suggest we hire a car, but John shakes his head: "We'll take the bus, dad. They wouldn't understand if we came in a car."

Of course, in Ethiopia years ago, his mother and I did not have the luxury of renting a car either, nor would our villagers have understood if we arrived by Land Rover.

On the bus out of the capital, we travel through green, rolling country, passing the occasional small, tin-roofed house with a red dirt yard where children play football with deflated balls. When the bus stops, roadside vendors yell to catch our attention, holding up boxes of soda and candy.

At Caaquazu, three hours out of Asunción on the road to Brazil, we leave the bus again and unload our luggage. Colleen dashes to the *supermercado* while John negotiates with taxi drivers to take us the last sixteen kilometers to Sextilinnia, their village. At first, negotiations do not go well. The drivers protest. The road is impassable, they say. But my son's negotiating skills slowly overcome their reluctance and, finally, a driver agrees to give it a try.

Soon after leaving the paved streets of Caaquazu, we hit a deep sea of mud. Our driver swings past the pool, carving a new road across a field. We continue on, forging new tracks where necessary. We are halfway to Sextilinnia when the driver, his wheels churning hopelessly, surrenders: *"No mas,"* he sighs.

Fortunately, there is a truck nearby belonging to people John and Colleen know—John, in fact, is building a water system for the school in their village—and they agree to drive us the rest of the way.

The village of Sextilinnia has only five houses. Corn and manioc plants grow in the rich soil that John tells me is fifty meters deep, thanks to run-off from the Andes. Years ago, in an attempt at land reform, the government gave the *campesinos* forested land, some tools, and a bit of hope. Now the forests are nearly gone, and the Ministry of Agriculture failed in an effort to cultivate citrus trees. The grind of poverty and subsistence farming goes on and on.

We unload the truck and carry the luggage into the house. "We can't let the neighbors know we have all this," John says. "They wouldn't understand such wealth."

After they open their presents, they take me on a tour of their village. Up the hill is the school where Colleen teaches health classes and John has undertaken a construction project. Beyond the hill we visit families. "This woman just had twins," Colleen explains, pointing to one house. "That was a month ago. I got her to the clinic in time to save the second child and the mother." She smiles sadly, remembering the event. "This is my work," she whispers.

And then my son continues, "Their father is my counterpart. He's a hoot. A strong leader. I took him into Asunción for counterpart day a few months ago, and he was so distracted he forgot to pay the school electric bill. That might cost him the PTA presidency," he explains, laughing.

We continue along the road, exchanging greetings with everyone who passes. Farmer after farmer. Family after family. We stop to talk with a strawberry farmer. "Too much rain, the crop is no good," he says as we sit under a barren citrus tree in his red earth patio. "But come see my latrine. I'm building it just like you said, away from the water well."

The two men stand on the mound of fresh earth and stare into the newly dug pit. Both voices speak with pride about the depth of the hole. We stay some time beneath the citrus tree. They talk of crops, children, the new school building, of health, of family, and of hope. The exchange is joyful, happy, boisterous, and good.

Later, back at the house, we sit on the porch, slapping ants that crawl up our legs and taking bets on when it will start to rain.

Eventually, it's time for bed and my son warns me, "Oh, if it rains really hard, you might want to move your bed over to that spot." He pointed across the room. "That's the only place in this room where it doesn't drip."

Shortly after midnight, a rooster is confused by the lightning and thunder and starts crowing. Down the hill another joins him. Soon roosters from the whole village are answering back.

At 5:45 a.m. the alarm rings. I knock on my son's door. Go back to sleep, he tells me. There will be no bus today. We'll have to walk to the main road.

When everyone is up, we shut down the house, load our packs, cover them with rubber rain gear and head off on the sixteen kilometer hike to Caaquazu and the bus to Asunción. It keeps raining and the mud gets deeper. There is no bus. No jeeps. Not even an ox-cart. The three of us trek on, keeping up our spirits by claiming to have the heaviest pack, to be the wettest. We stop at the house of another Peace Corps Volunteer, who offers us coffee and dry clothes. Like all Volunteers, thirty years ago and today, what we have, we share.

Back in the capital, we sit and talk most of the night.

We reform the Peace Corps, straighten out the Department of Interior where I work, we restructure the White House, as well as the Paraguayan government. There is no problem we can't solve.

Thirty years ago, my wife and I talked the same talk. We had solutions to the problems of Ethiopia, the United States, and the world. Now I wonder: Did we do any good as Peace Corps Volunteers in Ethiopia? Will John and Colleen do any good in Paraguay?

The answer, I think, is in the smiles and laughter of those we left behind in our highland village and in our own lives, and what we made of each day's work. The answer is also the children that we raised. For us, a son who cares enough about solving the problems of the world to join the Peace Corps. The answer is the work that Colleen and John are doing today in Paraguay—the same kind of work Patti and I did in Ethiopia thirty years ago.

There's a country-and-western song that says it best: May the circle be unbroken. That's the answer. May the circle of helping others go unbroken. In Paraguay, with my son and daughter-in-law, I realized I had come full circle. I had come home again to the Peace Corps.

John Garamendi (Ethiopia 1966-68) graduated from the University of California, Berkeley, where he was an All Pacific Coast Conference football player. After serving in the Peace Corps and earning an M.B.A. from Harvard University, he began a twenty-year legislative career in California. In 1995, he was appointed by President Clinton to serve as Deputy Secretary of the Interior.

Washington, D.C.

ROSE GARDEN REDUX
by John Coyne

A police escort with sirens blaring led our dozen Peace Corps buses in one long continuous caravan through every downtown light in Washington, D.C. It was high noon in the summer of 1962 and we—the 300 Ethiopia-bound Peace Corps trainees at Georgetown University—were on our way to meet John F. Kennedy at the White House.

There were others meeting the President as well. Peace Corps trainees at Howard, American, Catholic, and George Washington Universities, and the University of Maryland, over 600 in all, gathered in the August heat and humidity on the great lawn below the Truman Balcony.

I walked slowly up the hill with the Washington Monument behind me and the White House on the slight rise ahead, thinking how small the building was, no bigger than the country club where I had spent my summers as a caddy. I thought, too, of how lean Kennedy looked, standing at a raised podium with his one hand caught in the pocket of his dark suit jacket as he said, "From Georgetown University, 307 secondary school teachers for Ethiopia." He glanced up from the pages and smiled as he asked, "Perhaps those of you going to Ethiopia could hold up your hands."

We cheered, thrilled at being recognized by JFK.

We were the Peace Corps, the shiny new creation that he had proposed in the last days of the 1960 presidential campaign, his experiment in international development that others had called a wacky and dangerous idea. The Daughters of the American Revolution warned of a "yearly drain" of "brains and brawn...for the benefit of backward, underdeveloped countries." Former President Eisenhower declared it a "juvenile experiment," and Richard Nixon said it was another form of "draft evasion." The following year, *Time* magazine declared in a cover story that the Peace Corps was "the greatest single success the Kennedy administration has produced."

We thought so, and so did most Americans. Everyone, it seemed, was impressed by a "peace corps," the idea of Americans going out into the world to do good. That summer, all across the country, our names were read on our local news stations on the days we departed for training. We were front-page stories in newspapers as diverse as *The New York Times* and the *Kalamazoo Gazette*. We were on the evening news with Walter Cronkite, and Huntley and Brinkley.

On our first night in Washington, the Ethiopia trainees went en masse for a walk along the C & O Canal. The walk was led by Supreme Court Justice William O. Douglas, who had recently saved the canal by having it designated a historic monument. At the end of two miles, we stopped for hot dogs, beer, and an impromptu talk by a lanky kid named John D. Rockefeller IV, who was just back from studying in Asia and working at the Peace Corps headquarters. He later moved to West Virginia, where he became the governor and then a U.S. Senator.

At Georgetown University, we were up before dawn for calisthenics on the high ground behind the campus. On those mucky, hot mornings we were often joined by Harris Wofford, one of the architects of the Peace Corps and Special Assistant to the President for Civil Rights. He became our country director in Ethiopia, later a U.S. Senator, and now is head of the Corporation for National Service. Later in the day there were guest lectures by Under Secretary of State Chester Bowles; Special Assistant to the President Arthur Schlesinger, Jr.; and Walt Rostow of the National Security Council. They were just part of a gallery of academic and government officials who came to campus to prepare us for Ethiopia.

And now we were at the White House and John F. Kennedy was saying, "I hope that you will regard this Peace Corps tour as the first installment in a long life of service, as the most exciting career in the most exciting time, and that is serving this country in the sixties and the seventies."

Looking again at the old black-and-white photographs taken that afternoon, I see the President smiling down at the group of young women in bright flowery dresses, and young men with short haircuts, white shirts, narrow ties, and serious dark suits.

"The White House," Kennedy said, summing up, "belongs to all the people—but I think it particularly belongs to you."

I thought then that someone standing with me on that lawn might one day claim residence at 1600 Pennsylvania Avenue. I was wrong, but just barely. The late Paul Tsongas, who stood one row over from me in the Ethiopian group that summer afternoon, was the first former Volunteer to become a U.S. Senator and the first former Volunteer to run for President.

Then as Kennedy turned to leave the lawn, he stopped and asked us to write, to tell him how it was going. And he grinned and added, "But no postcards," referring to the famous postcard written by Nigeria Volunteer Margery Michelmore in October of 1961.

Michelmore, a twenty-three year-old *magna cum laude* graduate of Smith College, and one of the first people to apply to the Peace Corps, had written a postcard home to a friend describing in blunt terms the primitive living conditions in Ibadan. Her candor caused a diplomatic wildfire in Nigeria, and for several weeks her postcard was a *cause célèbre* in the United States. To the Ethiopia trainees that day, Kennedy's postcard reference showed not only his wit but also that he would be following our adventures overseas with interest. (Years later I learned that when Margery Michelmore arrived at Idlewild Airport in New York, having resigned from the Peace Corps, there was a handwritten note of sympathy waiting for her from the President.)

Kennedy said goodbye to us out there on the lawn and, with a nod, slipped his hand once more into the jacket pocket, and went back into the White House.

That was the last any of us would see of him.

We went overseas a few days later. We were the first great wave of Volunteers to fly to the ends of the earth and to the top of the world because John F. Kennedy had challenged us with a single sentence in his Inaugural Address: "And so, my fellow Americans, ask not what your country can do for you; ask what you can do for your country."

Nearly a thousand days later, far from that August afternoon in Washington, Ethiopian friends woke me after midnight with news of the assassination. I lay awake in the middle of Africa, in the middle of the night, with the only sound the hooting of hyenas scavenging near my dung-walled house, and I thought of that bright, sunny day at the White House and Kennedy with his chestnut hair and his lean frame and his right hand tucked into his suit pocket, turning away from us and asking us to write.

All of this came back to me again in June 1996 when I went to the White House for an event in the Rose Garden to celebrate the thirty-fifth anniversary of the Peace Corps. The members of "Ghana I," the first Volunteers to go overseas, the first to meet Kennedy in the Rose Garden, had been invited back by President Clinton. Also on hand were the newest group of Volunteers leaving for Ghana and a few dozen others like myself who had, in one way or another, been connected with the agency over the years. It was the first time I had been to the White House since that summer of '62.

Again, we gathered in the afternoon; again, it was humid in Washington. Unlike the first visit, when we hopped off buses and ambled up the lawns, this time we were screened by security at the East Gate, our photographs checked against our Social Security numbers, and then passed through metal detectors before finding ourselves on the grounds behind the White House, where we were handed an official program listing the speakers for the afternoon.

Looking down the hillside toward where the buses had parked, I realized that the open lawns I remembered were now all gone, landscaped with flowering shrubbery and trees. Also, I had always believed I had seen Kennedy in the Rose Garden. But now I was ushered past the spot where Kennedy had stood to address us in '62, around the White House, through white arches and into the actual Rose

Garden, which was a small enclosed patch of grass framed by high hedges and half-filled with rows of metal folding chairs.

The new Ghana trainees, thirty-nine of them, were already seated in front, facing a podium with the presidential seal. Watching them, I could not recognize myself in their bright, young faces. I remembered us as being much more intense and serious, wearing our dress-up clothes, filled with our own importance and the role we were about to enact in the Peace Corps. All of us now, the gray haired and middle-aged, were still wearing serious suits and dresses. In contrast, the new Ghana trainees, who had shaken hands individually with President Clinton in the Oval Office and posed there for photographs, were dressed like White House tourists, in khakis, with no ties, and short-sleeve shirts.

Glancing across the neat rows of chairs, I spotted George Carter, the first African American country director hired by Sargent Shriver. He went with the first group to Ghana and, after the Peace Corps, had a long career as an IBM executive.

Harris Wofford was there, too. With a handful of others, he had accompanied Shriver on an eight-country, twenty-six-day trip around the world in 1961 to sell the idea of the Peace Corps to potential host countries, beginning in Ghana with President Kwame Nkrumah.

Wofford came into the Rose Garden and began to shake hands with the returned Volunteers now serving in

Congress: Tony Hall from Ohio, who had served in Thailand; Tom Petri from Wisconsin, who had been in Somalia; Christopher Shays of Connecticut who, with his wife, Betsy, had served in Fiji; Jim Walsh of New York, who had served in Nepal; and Sam Farr of California, an early Volunteer in Colombia.

Also on hand were other returned Peace Corps Volunteers who were members of the Clinton administration, including Mary Jo Bane, Assistant Secretary of Health and Human Services, and John Garamendi, Deputy Secretary of the Interior. Solicitor General Drew Days sat a few seats in front of me. Beside me was the Deputy Director of the Peace Corps, Ambassador Charles Baquet, who had been a Volunteer in Somalia and, years later, U.S. Ambassador to the Republic of Djibouti.

For all of them, Kennedy had been right. Peace Corps had been their first installment in a long life of service, stretching from the sixties into the eighties and the nineties.

Then President Clinton came out of the Oval Office, walking with, and towering over, Sargent and Eunice Shriver, and Mark Gearan, Director of the Peace Corps. With them was Mandy Jackson, a young Ghana trainee who had been selected to speak for her group.

As we all stood, I was struck by how imposing President Clinton was, and how he worked the group with his eyes, nodding and smiling and waving to faces that he knew, while Mark Gearan read off the list of distinguished RPCVs in attendance: Gordon Radley, President of

LucasFilms; Elaine Jones, Director of the NAACP's Legal Defense and Education Fund; and television's Bob Vila.

Then it was time for Mandy Jackson of Madison, Wisconsin and Emory University to introduce the President. She did so, declaring, "Not only is it an honor to stand here before you today, but also I feel privileged to be a citizen of the United States. We are grateful for those whose support helps keep this special organization strong. President Clinton is one of those people."

The Peace Corps, President Clinton began, "symbolized everything that inspired my generation to service. It was based on a simple yet powerful idea: That none of us alone will ever be as strong as we can all be if we'll all work together."

His speech was longer than Kennedy's in 1962, and much more thoughtful. Where Kennedy had simply praised us, and his own idea, Clinton spoke of what was next for the agency. "I am proud to announce the establishment of a Crisis Corps within the Peace Corps to help the relief community to cope with international emergencies." I thought how Kennedy had spoken to us only of his hopes for the new venture, whereas Clinton came with a knowledge of the agency's thirty-five-year history. "Even as we meet, the Peace Corps is hard at work in countries few could have imagined going to back in 1961," he said. "Indeed, the Peace Corps is hard at work today in countries that did not exist in 1961."

He was right. Those of us who served in the sixties had

never imagined Volunteers serving as they have, in half the countries of the world, including new, post-Communist nations like Ukraine, Kyrgyz Republic, and Uzbekistan.

And to many of these young Volunteers, John F. Kennedy is just a president in their history books. The Peace Corps is an institution now, as solid as any of the capital's monuments.

It wasn't that way for us. In 1962 we didn't know if the Daughters of the American Revolution and the other critics of the Peace Corps might not be right. Our joining up with Kennedy's new venture might have meant a stain on our careers for the rest of our lives.

And yes, it was a dangerous idea, but not in the way the Daughters thought. The Peace Corps changed us. It made us aware of the world in ways we never would have been if we had stayed at home. Like Margery Michelmore in Ibadan, Nigeria, we were initially shocked by the conditions in which most of the world lives daily. We were innocent. We were naive. We went into the Peace Corps as the Silent Generation, but because of our experience, we came home knowing that the peoples of the world did go to bed hungry every night, and did not have the opportunities which we took for granted in America. The Peace Corps experience made us better citizens. It made us more involved and concerned about the welfare of the have-nots in our country and around the world. And it encouraged us to try to do something about it.

I wanted to lean forward and whisper to the fresh faces

that they hadn't seen anything yet, that sitting in the Rose Garden and being praised by the President was just a beginning.

But they wouldn't have understood. They had to experience Ghana and Africa. They had to come to terms with themselves in places that were not yet in the geography of their minds.

Earlier, Mandy Jackson had made us chuckle when she declared, "I suspect that I will learn as much as I teach." What Mandy suspected, we all knew.

Leaving the Rose Garden, I shook hands with Mandy and the other trainees and wished them good luck in Ghana.

I didn't tell them to write.

John Coyne (Ethiopia 1962-64) was with the first group of Volunteers to serve in Ethiopia and taught English in Addis Ababa. Later he was an Associate Peace Corps Director in Ethiopia and is now the Regional Manager of the New York Peace Corps Office. He is a novelist and editor of *Going Up Country: Travel Essays by Peace Corps Writers*, and the founding editor of *RPCV Writers & Readers*, a newsletter for and about Peace Corps writers.

Chile, South America

TO BE A VOLUNTEER
by Tom Scanlon

O n June 20, 1962, President John F. Kennedy greeted summer interns at the White House with a story
he had heard about a young Peace Corps Volunteer
named Tom Scanlon, who was serving in Chile.

"He works in a village about forty miles from an Indian
village which prides itself on being Communist," Kennedy told
his audience. "The village is up a long, winding road which
Scanlon has taken on many occasions to see the chief. Each
time, the chief avoided seeing him. Finally he saw him and
said, 'You are not going to talk us out of being Communists.'
Scanlon said, 'I am not trying to do that, only to talk to you
about how I can help.' The chief looked at him and replied, 'In

*a few weeks the snow will come. Then you will have to park
your Jeep twenty miles from here and come through five feet of
snow on foot. The Communists are willing to do that. Are
you?' When a friend saw Scanlon recently and asked him what
he was doing, he said, 'I am waiting for the snow.'*

*Recently, Tom Scanlon wrote his recollections of being one
of the first Peace Corps Volunteers. The following essay about
what it means to be a Volunteer is taken from his book,*
Waiting For The Snow.

—Editors

To be a Volunteer does not necessarily mean to endure
poor conditions. This is another way in which the Peace
Corps has been misunderstood. Many people believe that
to be in the Peace Corps, you must live in a slum. However,
one of the first pieces of advice which experienced people
gave us was not to live as the *campesinos* do. First of all,
conditions of life among *campesinos* are not only poor but
unhealthy; and they have resistance to cold, dampness, and
germs which we do not have. Secondly, it is not necessary
to live like a *campesino* to be accepted by the people; it is
necessary only to live simply, be yourself, and associate
with the *campesinos* as much as you can until they realize
that they are your main reason for coming down here.

To live like the poor has a romantic appeal at the beginning, but after two weeks the glamour wears off and you
become content with making just the sacrifices which are

necessary. I make no attempt to pretend I am poorer than I am, and the Peace Corps has never asked me to. All that seems unnecessary now. On a train I go first class because I like to read philosophy along the way. My first five days on vacation were spent in the most comfortable hotel in the area. I read, ate well, and took three showers a day. In Rio Negro, we live modestly in clean, healthy surroundings, and we frequently have a meal out when we feel that our reserves of vitamins are running low.

To be in the Peace Corps in Chile is to struggle with the language, and I think it is a real accomplishment of our group that now we can do business and conduct our work in Spanish. Frequently, I do not have to translate mentally before using a word; it just pops into mind and runs over my lips in Spanish. The other morning I awoke from a dream, as I have from thousands, and realized that all the characters in the dream were speaking Spanish. In fact, many of us now have a a reverse language problem and find ourselves stumbling around when we discuss our work in English. So many words dealing with our work were learned directly in Spanish that we must pause and think before remembering their English equivalents.

Another challenge is to adjust to a host of changes which affect our daily life. There are signs that I am adjusting to Chile now. More mail comes to me from within the country than from the outside. I have grown to expect wine at lunch and to linger for a long time over my meals. Yesterday morning, I caught myself putting hot peppers on my scrambled eggs, a cross-cultural act if I ever committed one.

The people who once seemed strange and far-off no longer appear so, and this is a sign of adjustment. The man who works on the road and lives in a shack beside it is a friend of mine. The truck drivers who sleep and live in their trucks have told me about their way of life. When a *campesino* comes into town walking his horse, covered by his long black *manta* which fits over his head and hangs down so that you can see only his ankles and head, I look closely because it could be someone I know.

Above all, adjusting to Chile has meant slowing down. Here you work at a much slower pace than in the United States, and if you appear too rushed, it is very possible to offend people. You have to be interested in more than work at hand—in the meal over which your business is conducted, in friendship and in lively (if idle) conversation. You must not raise a business matter for discussion immediately, or slice it up into organized pieces. Rather, you ease into the subject, talk by way of implication and leave everything in a half-organized state. "When will I travel here to meet you again?" You do not answer, "This Saturday, at four o'clock," but rather, "Sometime this weekend."

It is always a temptation to withdraw into the world of North American friends, North American magazines, and other Peace Corps Volunteers, and to hold back from the people in your community. You have to hold back something, but the moment you cease making the effort to learn more about Chile and to increase your span of Chilean friends, you have left the real spirit of the Peace Corps behind.

Tom Scanlon (Chile 1961-62) did cooperative development work as a Volunteer in Chile with the Institute for Rural Education. Scanlon is a graduate of the University of Notre Dame and has graduate degrees in philosophy and international relations from the University of Toronto and Columbia University, respectively. He has owned and managed Benchmarks, Inc., a consultant firm specializing in international development, for twenty-seven years.

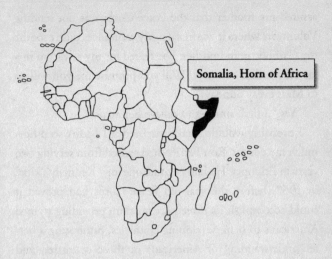

Somalia, Horn of Africa

FINDING MY VILLAGE
by Ambassador Charles R. Baquet III

"Are you crazy?" asked my father. "After all we sacrificed to put you through college, you're going to Africa to work for nothing?"

It was 1965 and I had just told my family that I was quitting my job as a social studies teacher in New Orleans to become a Peace Corps Volunteer in the Somali Republic. I assured my father that my college loan would be deferred and now he could get that new truck for his electrical business. When I completed two years, the Peace Corps would give me a readjustment allowance to pave my way into graduate school and jobs.

My mother worried about my health and safety, and I

assured my mother that the Peace Corps was not sending Volunteers where it wasn't safe. My assurances didn't soothe my Catholic grandmother. She feared for my salvation in a far-off Muslim country. "Will you promise me you will go to Mass every Sunday?"

"Yes," I lied, sinning to relieve her anxiety.

I probably wouldn't have persisted if I hadn't seen how much my cousin, Ron Ferrier, had gained from serving two years in Ethiopia. He had become one of "Kennedy's kids" in 1962, before the year-old Peace Corps had proved it could accomplish its three-part mission: providing trained Americans to help developing countries, promoting a better understanding of Americans in those countries, and giving Americans a better understanding of other people.

Besides, at twenty-five, I was restless. I longed to see the people and places I had read about in mission magazines as a child. I was in turmoil over the civil rights movement's conflicting methods, which ranged from the Rev. Martin Luther King's advocacy of non-violence to the Black Panthers' urban activism. I wanted distance to gain perspective.

And I did. My two years as a Peace Corps Volunteer helped me find my focus and led me to an exciting, satisfying career as a Foreign Service officer, an ambassador, and—completing the circle—the Deputy Director of the Peace Corps.

Nowadays when I urge African Americans to contribute two years of their energy and abilities, I tell them from first-hand knowledge that they will receive more than they give. Hundreds of the 148,000 Americans who have joined the Peace Corps since 1961 have told me this. They say it no matter where they served, or whether they volunteered in the idealistic 1960s, the cynical 1970s, the materialistic 1980s, or the rejuvenated 1990s.

My own life illustrates the point. My two-year assignment was to teach English and social studies at a boys' school in Erygavo, a village in northern Somalia. The British had built the school during their seventy-five-year colonial rule, and English was the language of instruction.

Soon after I arrived, a Somali asked me why I had come. "I am an African American and I came to find my village," I told him, proud of my profundity.

He laughed. "You're a fool. You have come all this way to find a village that doesn't exist. After 300 years, you are a different people than we are. There's a village for you some place. Find that place of peace in your heart and soul. There you will find your village."

I was devastated. I knew he was right. I had to turn within to find my village. His insight accelerated my search.

Teaching with few materials and living with no conveniences left little time for introspection. I shared half of a metal-roofed cement duplex with two other Volunteers, John Schecter from Wisconsin and Rozier Martin from Maine. They taught science and math, and the three of us ran the school. We had little in common except that we had all attended Catholic schools, but we became close friends.

They helped me ease my grandmother's fears. When we made the two-day trek to the nearest town, we found a priest but no Catholic church. He posed with me by a mosque that, at the right camera angle, looked like a church. I mailed the photos to my grandmother. Later, on leave in Kenya, I posed for photos with a man in dark robes in front of an Indian temple.

I knew those photos would comfort her more than hearing that the Somalis were ascetic, devout Sufi Muslims whose spirituality I admired.

Their diet of camel's milk, goat meat and rice, however, soon sent me to the cookbook in the bootlocker provided for each Volunteer household. I learned to cook goat meatloaf and lasagna outdoors on our charcoal brazier.

We missed vegetables. Forewarned by my cousin, I had brought a trunk stuffed with things I might need, including garden seeds. The Peace Corps tradition demands that you do more than your job, so growing vegetables became a special project. All went well until we left home for a few days. We returned to find goats had destroyed our sprouts. We suspected sabotage.

Another special project was stocking a library with books from discarded Peace Corps book lockers. When I went on vacation, the books disappeared. Students claimed ignorance.

Still another effort was providing recreation. My trunk held rope for making a volleyball net. We three Volunteers spent many hours figuring out the proper pattern and wove the net. The next time we were gone, the volleyball net vanished. Students said nomads had taken it.

When I completed my two years, I questioned whether I had really helped my students. In fact, until 1991, my Peace Corps experience seemed incomplete because all my special projects had failed. Yet I felt good about having managed a school and having been creative in solving problems. I came back feeling I could do anything.

Two weeks after I arrived in the United States, I was a program officer for VISTA, the domestic version of the Peace Corps. The Director was R. Sargent Shriver, the irrepressibly optimistic brother-in-law of President John F. Kennedy, who had chosen him to be the first Director of the Peace Corps.

In 1968, I started looking for a job in international development. President Lyndon Johnson urged the State Department to recruit minorities as career Foreign Service officers. Thanks to recommendations from embassy staff I had met in Somalia and from the Peace Corps, I became part of the first minority group to train for the Foreign Service under the President's Executive Order. My first assignment was the U.S. embassy in Paris. I've also served in Hong Kong, Beirut, Cape Town, Djibouti, and Washington, D.C. My assignments included a year at Syracuse University, where I earned a Master's degree, and a year in the Foreign Service Senior Seminar.

As Consul General in Cape Town from 1988 to 1991, I witnessed the end of apartheid in South Africa and the beginning of its constitutional process. I met the newly-released Nelson Mandela and many other remarkable people. I also saw the great contrasts between the cities and the countryside. I would not have hesitated, for example, to have open-heart surgery in Cape Town, but in rural areas I feared a cut.

Just when I thought my career couldn't be more fulfilling, President George Bush appointed me ambassador to Djibouti, a tiny former French colony in East Africa just northwest of my Peace Corps country. I felt I was going home. But this time, tribal warfare, drought, and famine plagued the area.

Word that a returned Peace Corps Volunteer had come back as ambassador spread quickly. Northern Somalis lined up outside my office, expecting "their" ambassador to perform miracles. The elders invited me back to Erygavo to assist with a peace and reconciliation conference of five tribes. The participants included some of my former students.

"We knew you of all people would be able to bring this reconciliation effort off," one said, and then he told me how he and other students had destroyed my garden, my library, and my volleyball net to see my reaction and what else I would pull from my trunk. I realized that even though my projects had not been successful, my work had left a lasting impression on my students. They realized as students that I had been there to help. They understood as adults that my efforts had brought them some measure of hope. At last, I thought, I had been a successful Volunteer after all.

But my connection to the Peace Corps would continue even after my time as ambassador to Djibouti. After he was elected in 1993, President Clinton nominated me to become Deputy Director of the Peace Corps. I hadn't sought the appointment, but I accepted immediately and with great enthusiasm. Since January 1994, in addition to representing the Peace Corps publicly, I spend much of my time recruiting the next generation of Volunteers from America's minority communities. I believe that the Peace Corps can fulfill its mission completely only if our Volunteers reflect the rich diversity of our nation. Today, about thirteen percent of Peace Corps Volunteers are minorities, and we hope to encourage more African Americans, Hispanic Americans, Native American and members of other minority communities to become a part of the Peace Corps experience.

I have also been fortunate to help establish the first Peace Corps project in South Africa. I led an assessment team that worked with eleven South African ministries and the president's office to create a program that would help meet the country's development needs. In February 1997, the first group of thirty-two Volunteers, ranging in age from twenty-two to sixty, arrived to begin training to address one of South Africa's greatest needs: primary education. Some rural schools don't own one book, and their pupils bring chairs from home or sit on the floor.

The Volunteers—sixty percent of whom are African, Asian, or Hispanic Americans—are working with teachers to develop teaching materials. After school, they help their communities build their capacity to provide such critical elements as clean water and basic health care. Combining education and community development is tough, and we chose those first Volunteers carefully.

One is Norma Harley, aged sixty, who had just returned from teaching as a Peace Corps Volunteer in Nepal. She rejected her daughter's suggestion of settling down in Sacramento and baby-sitting her grandchild. Norma told a reporter, "I've been optimistic in a lot of things that have happened in our country, coming through Martin Luther King's era and Malcolm X, and then let down in so many ways. And I really hope, in South Africa that they don't have to go through the disappointments."

Another is C.D. Glin, aged twenty-five, who put a Foreign Service opportunity on hold in order to become a Peace Corps Volunteer. He wrote anti-apartheid rap songs as a youngster and shook President Mandela's hand while attending Howard University in Washington, D.C. He was a leader of groups such as Concerned Black Men, a mentoring organization. He also tutored immigrants in English.

South Africa is a country that is rich in both natural and human resources. As always, the Peace Corps strives to work itself out of a job, which it has done now in more than thirty countries. If all goes well, the country will require Peace Corps assistance for no more than ten years.

Another program I am especially interested in is Haiti. My father's family came from Haiti to Louisiana in 1809, and my mother's family just before 1900. Haiti was the slave ships' last stop before the United States, and the place and people have the look of Africa. They are warm, hospitable, and hard working, and many of them are incredibly poor.

The Peace Corps program in Haiti was suspended in 1991 because of a military coup. But in 1996—after U.S. forces had helped restore democracy—Peace Corps Volunteers returned. In December, I went to Haiti to swear in a new group of Volunteers and visit the first group. Most are working with farm cooperatives to improve mango, avocado and papaya trees so that Haitians can raise commercially acceptable varieties to market abroad. Like modern Johnny Appleseeds, the Volunteers are grafting imported varieties onto the disease-resistant local trees. For example, Haitian-born Solange Lee, aged fifty-eight, holds a Master's degree in rehabilitation counseling from Hunter College and was the supervisor of a shelter for the homeless in Brooklyn. Christine Steinmann, a veterinarian in Arizona, had worked in Kenya. She is developing an animal husbandry program.

In each of these Volunteers and hundreds of others whom I have visited around the world since my return to the Peace Corps, I see the same sense of adventure, interest in other cultures and desire to do something meaningful that I felt when I served as Volunteer in the 1960s. This is the great genius of the Peace Corps—Americans serving our country by making a difference in the lives of other people. And just as I did when I found my village in Somalia, the men and women who are serving in the Peace Corps are laying the foundations for their future lives by finding their own inner villages now.

Charles R. Baquet III (Somali 1965-67) taught English and Social Studies at the Dayaha School in Erigavo and at the Hargeisa Girls School and Hargeisa Technical School in Hargeisa. Baquet received a B.A. in History and English Literature from Xavier University in New Orleans, and earned his M.A. in Public Administration from the Maxwell School of Government at Syracuse University. He has been a Foreign Service Officer for thirty-five years, posted in Paris, Hong Kong, Beirut, Cape Town (as Consul General), and served as Ambassador to Djibouti (1991-93) before his appointment as Deputy Director of Peace Corps.

Washington, D.C.

I STAND IN AWE
by Loret Miller Ruppe

L*oret Miller Ruppe was appointed the eleventh Director of the Peace Corps by President Ronald Reagan in 1981. During her distinguished eight-year tenure, Director Ruppe strengthened the Peace Corps in immeasurable ways, carried out an expansive vision of its role in the world, and provided strong support to Peace Corps Volunteers. She left the Peace Corps in 1989 as the longest-serving Director in the agency's history. After her death in 1996, Peace Corps Director Mark D. Gearan established the Loret Miller Ruppe Lecture Memorial Lecture Series, which provides a forum for prominent individuals to address important public policy issues that bear on the Peace Corps' mission. In 1997, the Peace Corps established the Loret Miller Ruppe Fund for the Advancement of Women, a cause to which she devoted much of her time and* *energies as Director of the Peace Corps.*

The following remarks are taken from her address at the Peace Corps' thirty-fifth anniversary celebration in Washington, D.C. on March 1, 1996.

—Editors

In 1983, I was invited to the White House for the state visit of Prime Minister Ratu Mara of Fiji. Everyone took their seats around an enormous table—President Reagan, Vice President Bush, Caspar Weinberger, the rest of the Cabinet, with the Prime Minister and his delegation, and myself. They talked about world conditions, sugar quotas, nuclear-free zones. The President asked the Prime Minister to make his presentation. A very distinguished gentleman, he drew himself up and said, "President Reagan, I bring you today the sincere thanks of my government and my people." Everyone held their breath and there was total silence. "For the men and women of the Peace Corps who go out into our villages, who live with our people." He went on and on. I beamed. Vice President Bush leaned over afterwards and whispered, "What did you pay that man to say that?"

A week later, the Office of Management and Budget presented the budget to President Reagan with a cut for the Peace Corps. President Reagan said, "Don't cut the Peace Corps. It's the only thing I got thanked for last week at the state dinner." The Peace Corps' budget went up. Vice

President Bush asked kiddingly again, "What did you pay?"

Well, we know one thing: it isn't for pay that Volunteers give their blood, their sacred honor. I can never forget the sweat, the tears, the frustrations, the best efforts and successes of thousands of Peace Corps Volunteers. I stand in awe and with the deepest respect. I always thought I could be a Volunteer until I went out and met them.

I ended many speeches when I was Peace Corps Director with this: Peace, that beautiful five-letter word we all say we crave and pray for, is up for grabs in the '90s. A question must be answered above and beyond this special forum: Is peace simply the absence of war? Or is it the absence of the conditions that bring on war, the conditions of hunger, disease, poverty, illiteracy and despair?

When fifty percent of the children die in a village before they are five; when women walk miles for water and then search for wood to cook by; when farmers leave their villages where there are no jobs to flock to cities where there are no jobs; when neighbors ethnically cleanse their neighbors, then let's face it, America, the world is not at peace.

And here at home, when fifty percent of our children live below the poverty level in many of our cities, when the homeless abound on our streets, when our nation's capital is bankrupt and our schools require metal detectors, racial tensions abound and immigrant bashing and downsizing terrorizes loyal workers, then, let's face it, America, we are not at peace.

The Peace Corps family must respond again to "Ask not what your country can do for you, rather ask what you can do for your country." And today, in our world, it is, as President Kennedy said, the "towering task." We can do it!

Loret Miller Ruppe received the Shriver Award for her outstanding work as Peace Corps Director from 1981-1989. She died in 1996.

APPENDICES

A History of the Peace Corps

October 14, 1960 — Presidential candidate John F. Kennedy addresses students at the University of Michigan at 2:00 a.m. in an impromptu speech, challenging them to give two years of their lives to help people in countries of the developing world. Inspired by the speech, students form "Americans Committed to World Responsibility" and organize a petition drive asking for the establishment of such a program; within weeks, more than 1,000 Michigan students have signed it.

January 20, 1961 — President Kennedy includes what becomes basic Peace Corps philosophy in his inaugural address: "To those peoples in the huts and villages of half the globe struggling to break the bonds of mass misery, we pledge our best efforts to help them help themselves . . ."

March 1, 1961 — President Kennedy issues Executive Order establishing the Peace Corps. Three days later, Sargent Shriver is appointed its first Director.

August 28, 1961 — President Kennedy hosts ceremony at the White House Rose Garden in honor of the first group of Peace Corps Volunteers departing for service in Ghana and Tanganyika (later Tanzania).

September 22, 1961 — Congress approves legislation formally authorizing Peace Corps, giving it the mandate to "promote world peace and friendship" through the following goals: (1) To help the people of interested countries and areas in meeting their needs for trained workers; (2) To help promote a better understanding of Americans on the part of the peoples served; and, (3) To help promote a better understanding of other peoples on the part of Americans.

December 1961 — By the end of the year, Peace Corps programs start up in Brazil, Chile, Colombia, Ghana, India, Malaysia, Nigeria, Pakistan, Philippines, St. Lucia, Sierra Leone, Tanzania, and Thailand. Total number of Volunteers reaches 750.

June 1962 — Programs begin in Afghanistan, Belize, Bolivia, Cameroon, Cyprus, Dominican Republic, Ecuador, El Salvador, Ethiopia, Iran, Ivory Coast, Jamaica, Liberia, Nepal, Niger, Peru, Somali Republic, Sri Lanka (Ceylon), Togo, Tunisia, Turkey, and Venezuela. As of June 30, 1962, there are 2,816 Volunteers in the field.

December 1963 — Programs begin in Costa Rica, Gabon, Grenada, Guatemala, Guinea, Honduras, Indonesia, Malawi, Morocco, Panama, Senegal, and Uruguay. As of June 30, 1963, there are 6,646 Volunteers in the field.

April 1964 — Peace Corps Partnership Program is started to provide a link between U.S. contributors and requests for project assistance from the overseas communities in which Peace Corps Volunteers serve.

June 1966 — More than 15,000 Volunteers are serving in the field, the largest number in Peace Corps history.

November 1974 — The first returned Peace Corps Volunteers (RPCVs) are elected to U.S. House of Representatives. Paul Tsongas of Massachusetts, who served as a Volunteer in Ethiopia from 1962 to 1964, and Christopher Dodd of Connecticut, who served as a Volunteer in the Dominican Republic from 1966 to 1968. Tsongas is elected to the U.S. Senate in 1978 and Dodd is elected in 1980.

December 1974 — Peace Corps programs are operating in sixty-nine countries, the largest number to date.

March 1, 1981 — President Reagan offers congratulations to the Peace Corps on the twentieth anniversary of Kennedy's executive order that established the agency.

June 2, 1981 — Celebration of the Peace Corps' twentieth anniversary is held in Washington, D.C. Peace Corps has had programs in eighty-eight countries; 97,201 Americans have joined the Peace Corps.

January 30, 1985 — The first Peace Corps Fellows Program is established at Teachers College/Columbia

University to recruit, prepare, and place returned Volunteers as teachers in the New York City public schools. In exchange for a two-year work commitment, the returned Volunteers are offered scholarships for graduate study.

September 19-20, 1986 — Nearly 5,000 returned Peace Corps Volunteers gather at the Washington Mall to celebrate the Peace Corps' twenty-fifth anniversary.

November 20, 1988 — The John F. Kennedy Library hosts a special Peace Corps remembrance of President Kennedy, twenty-five years after his death. At the event, Peace Corps archives, including voluminous Volunteer journals and other artifacts, are formally donated to the Library.

January 20, 1989 — Carrying the flags of more than sixty nations where Peace Corps Volunteers serve, a group of returned Volunteers and staff march for the first time in a presidential inaugural parade.

July 1989 — President Bush announces from Budapest that Peace Corps Volunteers will begin serving in Hungary, establishing the first Peace Corps program in an Eastern European country.

September 28, 1989 — Peace Corps Director Paul Coverdell announces the establishment of "World Wise Schools." The program matches Peace Corps Volunteers overseas with elementary and junior high classes in the United States in an effort to promote international awareness and cross-cultural understanding. By the late fall of 1989, more than 550 schools are participating in the unique education program.

June 15, 1990 — In a Rose Garden ceremony, President Bush praises "the group of talented Americans who are . . . to take leave of these shores and become the first Peace Corps Volunteers to serve in Eastern Europe." The 121 Volunteers meet with the President during their stopover in Washington, D.C. en route to Poland and Hungary.

March 1, 1991 — Peace Corps celebrates its thirtieth anniversary. More than 125,000 Americans have served as Volunteers in over 100 countries.

July 22, 1992 — The first group of Peace Corps Volunteers leaves for the former Soviet Union. These Volunteers will work in small business enterprise projects in Lithuania, Estonia, and Latvia.

June 12, 1993 — The first group of English teacher Volunteers leaves for China.

April 1994 — Peace Corps Partnership program celebrates its thirtieth anniversary. Over the course of its thirty years, the Peace Corps Partnership Program has supported nearly 3,500 projects in more than eighty developing countries.

August 11, 1995 — The U.S. Senate confirms Mark D. Gearan as the fourteenth Director of the Peace Corps.

December 4, 1995 — Director Mark Gearan sends Peace Corps Volunteers to the island of Antigua to help rebuild homes damaged or destroyed by Hurricane Luis. This pilot effort marks the first assignment of the "Crisis Corps," a new initiative that enables experienced Peace Corps Volunteers and returned Volunteers to provide short-term assistance in response to humanitarian crises and natural disasters.

March 1, 1996 — Peace Corps celebrates its thirty-fifth anniversary in Washington D.C., where more than 1,500 returned Volunteers attend a series of events to honor their service. Nearly 7,000 Volunteers are serving in ninety-four developing countries.

April 30, 1996 — Peace Corps Volunteers return to Haiti after a five-year absence.

May 1, 1996 — Peace Corps holds a two-day conference on international volunteerism in Washington D.C., where representatives from thirty-six volunteer organizations representing twenty-six countries plan joint ventures and discuss the future of volunteerism in the developing world.

June 19, 1996 — President Clinton honors the Peace Corps at a Rose Garden ceremony reuniting the first group of Volunteers who left for Ghana thirty-five years earlier with a new group of Volunteers about to leave.

December 16, 1996 — The comprehensive survey of returned Peace Corps volunteers is released, showing that ninety-four percent of those who volunteered would make the same decision again to join the Peace Corps. Seventy-eight percent of returned Volunteers continue to serve their communities in the United States once they return home, demonstrating the Peace Corps' significant "domestic dividend."

February 13, 1997 — In one of the United States' most tangible gestures of partnership with South Africa, thirty-one Peace Corps Volunteers depart for the first time to work with South African teachers, after a rousing farewell at Howard University featuring the Reverend Jesse Jackson.

April 30, 1997 — The first group of Volunteers depart for Jordan to work on small business development and ecotourism, primarily with women. First Lady Hillary Rodham Clinton, hosting a send-off at the White House, announces the creation of the Loret Miller Ruppe Fund for the Advancement of Women, named for the longest-serving Peace Corps director and a champion of women in development. Twenty-two of the twenty-nine Jordan Volunteers are women.

HOW TO BECOME A
PEACE CORPS VOLUNTEER

SKILLS NEEDED FOR
PEACE CORPS PROGRAMS

Agriculture

Two or four year degree, or two to five years experience.

Agribusiness	Agriculture Education
Agronomy	Animal Husbandry
Crop Extension	Environmental Education
Fisheries	Forestry
Parks and Wildlife Management	

Skilled Trades

Vocational/Technical Education or Industrial Arts degree, or two to five years professional experience.

Carpentry	Construction
Electrical Work	Machining
Masonry	Metal Working
Plumbing	

Professional Services
Two or four year degree, or two to five years experience.

Business Management	Cooperatives
Health Education	Hydrology
NGO Development	Nursing
Nutrition	Social Work
Water & Sanitation Engineering	

Education
Bachelor's degree or appropriate certification; experience preferred but not always required.

Biology	Chemistry
English/TEFL	Math
Physics	Primary Teacher Training
Special Education	Secondary Teacher Training

Applying to the Peace Corps can be exciting, but it can also be challenging. The application process involves essays, interviews, letters of recommendation, and medical and dental examinations. This guide will familiarize you with Peace Corps' screening and placement process. Please keep it with your application materials to help track your progress through the application process.

VOLUNTEER PROJECTS

Peace Corps programmers work closely with host-country agencies to develop projects and identify Volunteer assignments. Peace Corps recruitment offices then identify the best candidates for the skills needed by host countries.

TIMING OF REQUESTS

Requests for Volunteers are grouped into four "seasons" according to when Volunteers report to pre-departure orientation prior to leaving the U.S. for their overseas assignments. The seasons are as follows:

Fall:	October - December
Winter:	January - March
Spring:	April - June
Summer:	July - September

The recruitment and placement process begins up to nine months prior to departing for an assignment overseas. For example, a Volunteer who begins training during the spring will likely have begun the application process during the previous fall.

Approximately two candidates are identified for each Volunteer requested; thus, the selection process is competitive.

The entire process—from submission of the application to arrival in country for pre-service training—will likely take six to nine months depending on when you apply, your technical skills, medical and legal eligibility, and the seasonal demand for Volunteers with your skills. Couples may take up to twelve months.

THE APPLICATION PROCESS

There are three major steps in the application process. Each step is described in the sections that follow.

- Application
- Nomination
- Invitation

STEP I: APPLICATION

APPLICATIONS ARE REVIEWED

Upon receiving your application, your Recruiter will send you a confirmation-of-receipt letter. Your Recruiter will then review your application to determine if your skills and interests in an assignment area match those requested by Peace Corps programs overseas.

All requests for Volunteers are grouped into forty assignment areas in five programming categories:
- Agriculture and Environment
- Business
- Education (math, science, and vocational)
- Health and Community Services
- TEFL (Teaching English as a Foreign Language)

Please review the Peace Corps Programs and Requirements booklet for a description of the educational background and/or experience needed to qualify for a particular assignment area.

Your application will not be considered if any of the following apply to you:
- you are not a U.S. citizen;
- you are under eighteen-years old;
- you are under supervised probation;

- you are or have been involved with intelligence orga
  nizations;
- you have dependents;
- your particular skills do not match those requested by
  Peace Corps host countries.

Recruiters will schedule an interview with applicants who
meet the requirements for the assignment areas currently
requested by Peace Corps programs overseas.

APPLICANTS ARE INTERVIEWED

The interview with your Recruiter usually takes place within two weeks of receipt of your application. Most applicants are interviewed in person; others may arrange interviews by phone. During the interview your Recruiter will
explore your flexibility, adaptability, social sensitivity, cultural awareness, motivation, and commitment to Peace
Corps service. Your Recruiter will not nominate you to an
assignment area without an expression of genuine commitment on your part to Peace Corps service.

In addition to meeting the requirements for an assignment area and completing the interview, there must be a current request for Volunteers with your skills and experience at the time you are available for Peace Corps service. If there is a request, you would then compete with candidates with similar skills applying to the same recruitment office.

APPLICANTS ARE NOMINATED

If you are selected to fill a current request, you will be "nominated" by your Recruiter for a specific assignment area and season of departure. A nomination means that your Recruiter formally places your name into consideration for one of many assignments for Volunteers with your skills and experience. You must still compete with nominees from other recruitment offices around the country for assignments in specific countries.

MEDICAL ASSESSMENT

You must be assessed medically and dentally by the Office of Medical Services in Washington, D.C. prior to Peace Corps service. The assessment is to ensure that you can perform your assignment without risk to your health. All medical information is kept confidential.

The Report of Medical History form submitted with your application remains sealed until you are nominated. The assessment process may be delayed or your placement options limited or eliminated altogether if you have certain medical conditions which may jeopardize your health while overseas. Please review the Medical Information for Applicants sheet to assess your chances of being medically cleared. If you have questions prior to nomination, please contact your Recruiter.

THINGS TO DO DURING THE APPLICATION PHASE

- Submit the application, the Report of Medical History form, a copy of your transcripts, and a copy of your resumé to the nearest recruitment office.
- Respond to the request to schedule an interview as soon as possible.
- Keep copies of all application materials.

Date Application Mailed: _____

Recruiter's Name: _____

Recruiter's Phone No.: _____

STEP 2: NOMINATION

APPLICANTS ARE NOTIFIED OF NOMINATION

If you are nominated to an assignment area, your Recruiter will notify you by mail and provide you with your assignment area number and title, and the season of departure (e.g., AA100 Forestry, Spring 1997).

At the time you are nominated, your Recruiter may be able to tell you the geographic region(s) (i.e., Africa; Europe, Asia, & the Mediterranean; Inter-America & the Pacific) with openings for your assignment area, but will not be able to tell you the specific country. Specific country assignments are determined during the invitation phase of the application process. Also, remember that host countries request Volunteers up to twelve months prior to pre-service training. Thus, assignments are subject to change, sometimes at the last minute.

Along with the letter confirming your nomination, your "nomination kit" will contain reference forms and envelopes, an update questionnaire, and forms for completing fingerprints and the applicant background investigation. Please review the materials carefully and contact your Recruiter if you have any questions. All forms must be completed promptly and forwarded to the Office of Placement in Washington D.C. in the envelope provided.

REFERENCES

In order to fully assess your qualifications for Peace Corps service, you will be required to submit four references, one each from the following categories:

- current/most recent work supervisor
- volunteer supervisor
- professor, advisor, or counselor
- personal acquaintance or co-worker

Mail or hand-deliver the reference forms to your references as soon as possible. Stress the importance of completing the forms thoroughly and returning them to you sealed and signed across the back of the envelope. Once you have collected all four references, you will forward them to the Office of Placement. Please contact your Placement Officer in the Office of Placement if you are having difficulties collecting your four references.

FINGERPRINT/BACKGROUND CHECK

All applicants are required to submit to a thorough background investigation as part of the application process. Fingerprints may be done at the local Peace Corps recruitment office at the time of your interview or after you have been nominated. Many police stations and state Departments of Motor Vehicles will also fingerprint applicants, but may charge a small fee.

MEDICAL HISTORY IS REVIEWED

Your Recruiter will forward your sealed medical package to the Office of Medical Services (OMS) as soon as you are nominated. A member of the OMS medical screening team will review your completed Medical History form shortly after it arrives in OMS. A medical examination packet will then be mailed to most applicants. A very small number of applicants may be deferred or medically disqualified from Peace Corps service based on information in their Medical History form. All applicants who receive the medical examination packet must undergo physical and dental examinations using the forms in the packet.

The results of the medical and dental examinations must be reviewed by OMS before an applicant can receive medical and dental clearance. It is your responsibility to provide all information required to determine your medical suitability for Volunteer service. Medical and dental processing time can be shortened by submitting complete and thorough information as quickly as possible. When known, please include the dates of events or conditions.

Medical and dental problems that could hinder your performance as a Volunteer must be resolved before you can be invited to serve in a specific assignment and country. The Peace Corps will reimburse the cost of medical and dental examinations up to prescribed limits based on age, gender, and other factors. However, the Peace Corps cannot pay for corrective health procedures or special evaluations.

LEGAL INFORMATION IS REVIEWED

Only applicants who meet the legal standards of eligibility established by Congress and the Peace Corps may be invited to enter pre-service training for a Volunteer assignment. If any of the legal issues listed below apply to you, your application will be reviewed by the Legal Liaison in the Office of Placement. Please note that the following circumstances do not necessarily disqualify you from Peace Corps service but will require clarification and documentation before the Legal Liaison can make a determination of your eligibility for Volunteer service:

- common law marriage
- married, serving without spouse
- divorce
- dependents
- previous convictions
- student loans
- financial obligations (e.g., home mortgage payments, child support)
- bankruptcy
- association with intelligence activity
- current obligations to the military

APPLICANTS ARE EVALUATED

Once you are nominated, your Recruiter will forward your application and a summary of your interview to the Office of Placement. Your Placement Officer will then review your application, references, and other supporting documents to verify that your technical skills and experience match those needed for the assignment to which you have been nominated. Your Placement Officer will also assess your suitability for Volunteer service using motivation, commitment, emotional maturity, social sensitivity, and cultural awareness as assessment criteria. If you meet the skill requirements and suitability assessment criteria for Volunteer service, your Placement Officer will consider you for assignments in a specific country.

The evaluation process, including medical and legal screening generally takes six to eight weeks from the date of receipt of your references, fingerprint and background investigation forms by the Office of Placement and your medical examination by the Office of Medical Services. If you have not submitted these forms, or your application has been placed on hold for medical or legal reasons, the evaluation process may be delayed.

THINGS TO DO DURING THE NOMINATION PHASE

• Contact references and urge them to complete the reference forms as soon as possible.

• Mail all four references, completed fingerprints and background investigation forms, and the update questionnaire to the Office of Placement within thirty days of receipt of your nomination kit.

• Complete the medical and dental examinations as soon as possible.

• Respond to all requests for additional medical, legal, and other information.

• Contact your Placement Officer if there are changes in your address, phone number, or other relevant information.

STEP 3: INVITATION

Applicants are invited to serve in a specific assignment and country. If your Placement Officer determines that you meet the general suitability and skill requirements for the assignment to which you have been nominated, and you have cleared both the medical and legal screening processes, your application will be assessed against country-specific criteria.

Placement Officers make the final decision whether to invite an applicant to begin pre-service training for a specific country and assignment. The placement process is competitive and is designed to ensure that Peace Corps Volunteers have not only the technical skills needed, but also the personal qualities necessary to work successfully in a specific assignment.

If you receive an invitation, you will have 10 days to respond. In addition to the letter of invitation, the invitation packet includes a Volunteer Assignment Description (VAD) to help you make the decision whether to accept the assignment. Also included are passport and visa applications, a request for an updated resumé, and an invitation handbook to guide you in preparing for departure.

If you have not heard from the Office of Placement thirty days after submitting your references and other materials, you should contact your Placement Officer to check the status of your application.

Once you have accepted an invitation, Peace Corps will send you additional information to help you prepare for departure. The Country Desk Officer for your country of assignment will send you a packet of information about your host country and a description of your pre-service training. The packet will include a recommended list of clothing and other items to take with you overseas and a country-specific bibliography.

Approximately four weeks prior to departure, you will receive reporting instructions with the date and location of your pre-departure orientation. The Travel Office will send you airline tickets and soon you will be on your way!

THINGS TO DO DURING THE INVITATION PHASE

• Respond to the invitation within 10 days.

• Contact the appropriate Placement Skill Desk at (800) 424-8580, press "2" (extensions below) if there are changes in your address, phone number, availability date, or other relevant information.

Agriculture	ext. 2216
Business	ext. 2253
Education	ext. 2238
Health/Community Services	ext. 2235
TEFL	ext. 2213

Placement Officer's Name: _____

Assignment Area: _____

Date Invitation Received: _____

Date Invitation Accepted: _____

COUNTRIES WHERE PEACE CORPS VOLUNTEERS ARE SERVING AS OF SEPTEMBER 1997

AFRICA
Benin

Botswana

Burkina Faso

Cameroon

Cape Verde

Chad

Côte d'Ivoire

Eritrea

Ethiopia

Gabon

The Gambia

Ghana

Guinea

Guinea-Bassau

Kenya

Lesotho

Madagascar

Malawi

Mali

Mauritania

Namibia

Niger
Senegal
South Africa
Tanzania
Togo
Uganda
Zambia
Zimbabwe

ASIA AND THE PACIFIC

China
Fiji
Kiribati
Micronesia
Mongolia
Nepal
Niue
Republic of Palau
Papua New Guinea
Philippines
Solomon Islands
Sri Lanka
Thailand
Tonga
Tuvalu
Vanuatu
Western Samoa

CENTRAL AND SOUTH AMERICA
Belize
Bolivia
Chile
Costa Rica
Ecuador
El Salvador
Guatemala
Guyana
Honduras
Nicaragua
Panama
Paraguay
Suriname

THE CARIBBEAN
Antigua & Barbuda
Dominica
Dominican Republic
Grenada
Haiti
Jamaica
St.Kitts-Nevis-Anguilla
St. Lucia
St. Vincent-Grenadines

EASTERN AND CENTRAL EUROPE

Armenia

Bulgaria

Estonia

Latvia

Lithuania

Former Yugoslav Republic of Macedonia

Moldova

Poland

Romania

Russia

Slovakia

Ukraine

CENTRAL ASIA/MIDDLE EAST/MEDITERRANEAN

Jordan

Kazakhstan

Kyrgyz Republic

Malta

Morocco

Turkmenistan

Uzbekistan

FORMER PEACE CORPS COUNTRIES

AFRICA
Burundi
Central African Republic
Comoros Islands
Democratic Republic of Congo (Zaire)
Equitorial Guinea
Liberia
Mauritius
Nigeria
Republic of Congo
Rwanda
São Tomé and Príncipe
Seychelles
Sierra Leone
Somalia
Sudan
Swaziland

ASIA AND THE PACIFIC
Bangladesh
Cook Islands
India
Indonesia
Marshall Islands
South Korea

SOUTH AMERICA AND THE CARIBBEAN

Anguilla

Argentina

Barbados

Brazil

Colombia

Montserrat

Peru

Turks and Caicos

Uruguay

Venezuela

EASTERN AND CENTRAL EUROPE

Albania

Czech Republic

Hungary

CENTRAL ASIA/MIDDLE EAST/MEDITERRANEAN

Afghanistan

Bahrain

Cyprus

Iran

Libya

Oman

Pakistan

Tunisia

Turkey

Yemen